Welcome

It's that time of year again…time to savor the sweetness of another holiday season with *Country Woman Christmas 2005*! We've packed our annual keepsake edition chock-full of Yuletide traditions, tastes, treats and treasures for you and your loved ones.

You'll find a sleighful of do-it-yourself stocking stuffers and homespun gift ideas, a smorgasbord of mouth-watering family recipes, and blizzards of merry decorating and party tips.

We've also tucked in our traditional true-life memories and nostalgic stories, uplifting seasonal poetry and profiles of country women who will inspire you with their creative ideas for celebrating the holidays at home.

So settle back, throw another log on the fire, and gather with family and friends to reflect, reminisce and rejoice in all the magic of an old-fashioned country Christmas. Then, until next year's new edition, enjoy our heartfelt wishes for peace, promise and goodwill to last a lifetime!

Executive Editor
Kathy Pohl

Editor
Mary C. Hanson

Food Editor
Janaan Cunningham

Art Director
Emma Acevedo

Assistant Food Editor
Karen Wright

Home Economist/Food Stylist
Joylyn Trickel

Senior Recipe Editor
Sue A. Jurack

Recipe Editor
Janet Briggs

Craft Editor
Jane Craig

Associate Editor
Mary Spencer

Proofreader
Kris Krueger

Editorial Assistant
Joanne Wied

Test Kitchen Assistant
Rita Krajcir

Food Stylists
Kristin Arnett, Sarah Thompson

Studio Photographers
Rob Hagen, Dan Roberts

Set Stylists
Sue Myers, Julie Ferron

Graphic Art Associates
Ellen Lloyd, Catherine Fletcher

President
Barbara Newton

Editor in Chief
Catherine Cassidy

Chairman and Founder
Roy Reiman

©2005 Reiman Media Group, Inc.
5400 S. 60th Street
Greendale WI 53129

International Standard Book Number:
0-89821-450-5
International Standard Serial Number:
1093-6750

PICTURED ON OUR COVER. Savor
the season with our Linzer Tart with angel cutouts (p. 34), Holly Butter Mints (p.
48) and Mocha Truffle Cups (p. 47) or
get creative with Napkin Ring Party Favors (p. 110), Paper Star-Flowers (p. 91)
or a Gala Glass Centerpiece (p. 53).

Contents

...and Much More!

She Trims a Christmas Wonderland with Treasures of the Heart

THERE'S NO PLACE LIKE HOME for the holidays…especially when it's trimmed from top to bottom, front door to back, with gay garlands, sentimental keepsakes and rooms full of Christmas collectibles and family treasures.

Just a peek inside the warm Sandusky, Ohio home of Sandra Reiber and husband Bob brings back a rush of the memories and magic that make this season so very special to their family—and to families everywhere.

"Christmas is my very favorite time of year," Sandra says simply, "and decorating for it is a kind of passion with me."

And a major production! It takes her a good month, working nights and weekends, to fix all the elaborately detailed "scenes" that nestle in each room and brighten every corner.

In the foyer, for instance, a woodlands scene complete with hiking Santa, wooden reindeer and three trees decked with birds and "chirping lights" greets visitors. A wreath made by daughter Traci hangs just inside, and a merry Mr. and Mrs. Claus beam from a hooked rug covering the closet door.

"That's special because it was made by my mother," Sandy explains. "She's 85 now, but she always decorated every inch of our house when I was growing up. She's my inspiration."

It all begins with the living room tree. Strung with apple garlands and clusters, special mementos from vacation trips and at least 50 different Santas, it's spectacular. One section holds only Nativity ornaments and angels, another boasts celebrity trims from favorite family movies and TV shows—Peanuts, Disney and Looney Tunes characters, *I Love Lucy*, *The Wizard of Oz* and sports ornaments for her husband.

And of course, there are those priceless trims made by the couple's three children decades ago…

Magical Memories

"I was finishing the tree late one night a few years back, when our oldest son came in," Sandra relates. "Holding out a

A MANTEL MERRY with her many Raggedy Ann and Andy collectibles and snow globes warms Sandra's family room hearth every Christmas.

little red felt figure with a white button eye, I said, 'Oh, David…look at this cute bear Eric made when he was little.'

"A grown-up David answered a bit stiffly, 'That's *not* a bear, it's Santa Claus, and *I* made it, not Eric'."

She chuckles at the memory. "That little ornament is the last one I hang on the tree every year…and the *first* one David looks for when he comes in…still!"

Beneath the tree, an old Lionel train chugs its way around the snowy track, station and figures tucked under the branches. Close by, a stack of favorite Christmas books is grouped with some of the close to 100 Santa figures Sandra has collected for years and scatters all through the house.

Over on a cocktail table, a rustic creche made by her father houses the creamy white figures Sandra made in a ceramics class years ago. And covering the entire piano is a lit and twinkling "city village" scene spread over snowy batting.

"I mix Department 56, Snow Village, Dickens, and other collectible pieces and figures with things meaningful to me that tell our holiday story," Sandra explains.

An equally detailed "country village" scene fills the dining room table and includes lighthouses, lodges, a lake, river and ♂

NOEL NOSTALGIA is celebrated in the elaborate old-time "city village" that covers the living room piano and twinkles with lights. A toy train circles the large tree filled with ornaments recalling family-favorite films and vacation memories. "It really is a joy to trim," Sandra says.

STAR-SPANGLED SANTAS strut across a table (above) with patriotic purpose. Sandra's lifetime collection of nearly 100 St. Nick figures is scattered throughout every room. The jolly old elf also decks the family tree (at right).

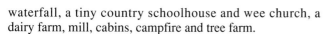

waterfall, a tiny country schoolhouse and wee church, a dairy farm, mill, cabins, campfire and tree farm.

Sandra still remembers 5-year-old grandson Austin standing spellbound before the amazing snowy scene and whispering, "Grandma, this is awesome. I wish I lived in there."

"He makes all the work worthwhile—a joy to do," she laughs.

Over in the family room, Sandra's cherished collection of Raggedy Ann and Andy dolls takes center stage and spills over the garland-draped mantel and fireplace.

"I have such fun putting that scene together and watching it grow each year with newfound treasures," she notes. "Those dolls bring back a lot of childhood memories for many folks." Nearby, an end table holds her collection of snow globes, and more Santas, bears and colorful throws brighten the couches and chairs in that room. There's even a holiday sports scene for former coach Bob's easy-chair corner!

"Lots of people hear about our decorations and stop by to see 'the Christmas house'," Sandra says. "And since I remember such magical Christmases when I was a child, sharing it all with others is a way to pass that magic on…and at least half the fun of the holidays!" ❄

CHRISTMAS BLESSINGS on the heroes of September 11, 2001 is the sentiment of the framed print (right). A gift from Sandra's daughter, Traci, it's brought out every Yuletide and is a cherished family treasure.

ADRIFT IN DREAMS, Sandra's vintage "country village" sprawls across the dining room table—and all its leaves! The whimsical winter wonderland glitters with lights and snow and celebrates the magic of Christmases long, long ago. It's a holiday favorite with all the Reiber grandkids.

There'll Always Be a Christmas

There'll always be a Christmas
As long as there is love,
As long as we commemorate
The Christ Child from above;

As long as there are gifts to give
And sparkling Christmas lights,
Mistletoe and holly,
And starry winter nights;

As long as the story is told
Of the Christ Child's humble birth;
As long as we sing *Silent Night*,
And pray for peace on Earth.

There'll always be a Christmas,
Whatever else we do,
To celebrate our Savior's birth—
God's gift to me and you!

—*Ruth Norsworthy Crager*
State Line, Mississippi

HE MAY BE "dressed all in fur from his head to his foot" or clad in red or white. He could be fat or thin and carrying twigs or toys. But whether you know him as Father Christmas, Kris Kringle, Belsnickel, Sinter Klaas or jolly old St. Nick…

Santa Claus has been bringing together children of all ages and nationalities—through generations of holidays—for one merry, magical night each year. Here, our staff shares some favorite renderings of this "jolly old elf" with you.

Jingle Bell Brunch

SCRUMPTIOUS SPREAD. Pictured clockwise from top right: Funshine Drink (p. 14), Souffle Roll-Up (p. 14), Festive French Pancakes (p. 14), Strawberry Pastries (p. 14) and quick, colorful Kiwi Dressing for Fruit (p. 15).

Wake up sleepyheads still nestled in bed with a rise-and-shine bounty of breakfast delights and a frosty bell-ringer beverage.

FESTIVE FRENCH PANCAKES
Diane Aune, Sacramento, California
(Pictured on page 12)

Not quite as thin as true crepes, these light-as-a-feather pancakes are topped with preserves and a dusting of confectioners' sugar. They're elegant, so easy to make and say "Joyeux Noel" with delicious French flair!

  2/3 cup milk
  2 eggs
  1/3 cup water
  1/2 teaspoon vanilla extract
  3/4 cup all-purpose flour
  2 tablespoons confectioners' sugar
  1 teaspoon baking powder
  1/2 teaspoon salt
Preserves of your choice, optional
Additional confectioners' sugar, optional

In a blender, combine the milk, eggs, water and vanilla; cover and process until well blended. Combine the flour, confectioners' sugar, baking powder and salt; add to egg mixture. Cover and process until smooth.

Pour batter by 1/4 cupfuls into a greased 8-in. skillet. Lift and tilt pan to coat bottom. Cook over medium heat until top appears dry; turn and cook 10-20 seconds longer. If desired, spread preserves over pancakes; roll up. Sprinkle with confectioners' sugar if desired. **Yield:** 8 pancakes.

FUNSHINE DRINK
Heather Campbell, Lawrence, Kansas
(Pictured on page 13)

My kids are crazy about this frosty, frothy drink any time of year. But I have to admit, the fresh fruity beverage is as welcome as a splash of winter sunshine with grown-up holiday guests, too.

  2 cups chilled orange juice
  2 cups chilled pineapple juice
  3 cups orange sherbet
  1 cup chilled club soda

In a blender, combine the juices and sherbet; blend until smooth. Stir in soda. Serve immediately. **Yield:** 8 servings.

STRAWBERRY PASTRIES
June Formanek, Belle Plaine, Iowa
(Pictured on page 12)

I found this recipe in an old cookbook and just love it. When our large family was home, I couldn't keep up with the demand for these yummy little pastries—the kids ate them as fast as I could bake them! It simply wouldn't be Christmas breakfast without a platter of these family favorites.

  1 package (1/4 ounce) active dry yeast
  1/4 cup warm water (110° to 115°)

  1 teaspoon plus 1/4 cup sugar, *divided*
  1 cup warm milk (110° to 115°)
  6 tablespoons shortening
  1 teaspoon salt
  1 egg
3-1/4 to 4 cups all-purpose flour
FILLING:
  1/4 cup sugar
1-1/2 teaspoons quick-cooking tapioca
  1/2 cup frozen sliced sweetened strawberries with juice, thawed
  1/2 teaspoon lemon juice
Melted butter
ICING:
  2 tablespoons shortening
  2 tablespoons butter, softened
  1 cup confectioners' sugar
  2 to 3 teaspoons milk
  1/4 teaspoon vanilla extract

In a large mixing bowl, dissolve yeast in warm water. Add 1 teaspoon sugar; let stand for 5 minutes. Add the milk, shortening, salt, egg, remaining sugar and 2 cups flour; beat until smooth. Stir in enough remaining flour to form a soft dough (dough will be sticky). Do not knead. Cover and refrigerate for 8 hours or overnight.

For filling, combine the sugar and tapioca in a saucepan; add strawberries. Let stand for 5 minutes. Bring to a boil; cook and stir for 2 minutes or until thickened. Stir in the lemon juice. Cool.

Punch down dough; divide in half. On a lightly floured surface, roll each portion to 1/4-in. thickness. Cut into 2-in. squares. Spoon about 1/2 teaspoon of filling into the center of each square. Bring two opposite corners together over center of filling; pinch to seal. Place 2 in. apart on greased baking sheets. Cover and let rest for 15 minutes.

Bake at 425° for 8-10 minutes or until golden brown. Remove to wire racks. Brush with melted butter; cool. For icing, in a small mixing bowl, cream the shortening and butter. Gradually beat in confectioners' sugar, milk and vanilla. Drizzle over pastries. **Yield:** 2-1/2 dozen.

SOUFFLE ROLL-UP
Esther Petschke, Fairmont, Minnesota
(Pictured on page 13)

Here's a "party pretty" omelet roll, topped with zesty mustard sauce, that offers make-ahead convenience on busy Yuletide mornings. Best of all, I can be sure everyone's ham and eggs will be hot and ready at exactly the same time!

  2 tablespoons all-purpose flour
  1/2 cup mayonnaise
  12 eggs, *separated*
  1 cup milk
  1/2 teaspoon salt
  1/8 teaspoon pepper
1-1/2 cups finely chopped fully cooked ham
  1 cup (4 ounces) shredded Swiss cheese
  1/3 cup minced fresh parsley

1/4 cup chopped green onions
PARSLEY SAUCE:
   1/2 cup minced fresh parsley
    2 garlic cloves, minced
    1 teaspoon minced fresh basil
   1/2 teaspoon sugar
   1/4 teaspoon salt
   1/8 teaspoon pepper
    1 tablespoon cornstarch
1-1/2 cups heavy whipping cream
    1 tablespoon Dijon mustard
MUSTARD SAUCE:
    1 cup mayonnaise
    2 tablespoons chopped green onion
    4 teaspoons prepared mustard

Line a 15-in. x 10-in. x 1-in. baking pan with waxed paper; grease the paper and set aside. In a saucepan, combine flour and mayonnaise until smooth. In a large bowl, whisk the egg yolks until thickened; add milk, salt and pepper. Whisk into mayonnaise mixture; cook over medium-low heat until slightly thickened, about 7 minutes. Remove from the heat; cool for 15 minutes.

In a large mixing bowl, beat egg whites until stiff peaks form. Gradually fold into mayonnaise mixture. Spread into prepared pan. Bake at 375° for 20 minutes or until golden brown. Run a knife around edges to loosen; invert onto a kitchen towel. Gently peel off waxed paper. Combine the ham, cheese, parsley and onions; sprinkle over souffle to within 1 in. of edges. Roll up from a short side. Place on a greased baking sheet. Cover and refrigerate until completely cooled, about 2 hours or overnight.

In a blender or food processor, combine the parsley sauce ingredients; cover and process until almost smooth. Cover and refrigerate for 1 hour or overnight. In a small bowl, combine mustard sauce ingredients; refrigerate until serving.

To reheat souffle, cover and bake at 375° for 40-50 minutes or until heated through. In a small saucepan, heat parsley sauce over medium heat until mixture comes to a boil, stirring constantly; cook and stir 1 minute longer. Cut souffle with a serrated knife; serve with parsley sauce and mustard sauce. **Yield:** 8 servings (about 2 cups parsley sauce and 1-1/4 cups mustard sauce).

Editor's Note: Reduced-fat or fat-free mayonnaise is not recommended for this recipe.

KIWI DRESSING FOR FRUIT
Edna Hoffman, Hebron, Indiana
(Pictured on page 12)

Looking for a way to make fresh fruit salad as special as Christmas morning itself? Give it a whirl with this blender-quick dressing drizzled on top.

   1/4 cup white grape juice
   1/4 cup vegetable oil
1-1/2 teaspoons lime juice
    2 kiwifruit, peeled and quartered
Dash salt
Assorted fresh fruit

In a blender, combine the grape juice, oil, lime juice, kiwi and salt; cover and process until smooth. Serve with fruit salad. **Yield:** 1 cup.

WHITE CHOCOLATE BERRY MUFFINS
Mary Lou Wayman, Salt Lake City, Utah
(Pictured above)

Santa himself might stop by just to get a taste of these rich moist muffins studded with white chocolate chips and juicy raspberries. They're sure to brighten any table.

    1 package (8 ounces) cream cheese, softened
    1 cup sugar
    2 eggs
    1 teaspoon vanilla extract
1-1/2 cups all-purpose flour
    2 teaspoons baking powder
   1/2 teaspoon salt
    1 cup fresh raspberries
   1/2 cup vanilla *or* white chips

In a large mixing bowl, beat cream cheese and sugar until smooth. Add eggs and vanilla; mix well. Combine the flour, baking powder and salt; add to cream cheese mixture just until blended. Stir in raspberries and chips.

Fill greased or paper-lined muffin cups two-thirds full. Bake at 375° for 20-25 minutes or until a toothpick comes out clean. Cool for 5 minutes before removing from pan to a wire rack. **Yield:** 1 dozen.

Muffin Tips

Muffins (and quick breads) are made with baking powder or baking soda instead of yeast. Ready to bake in minutes during busy holidays, they make wonderful homemade gifts. Some tips:
- Do not overmix, as this will toughen the texture.
- Do not overbake. Check doneness 10 minutes early.

OVEN-BAKED WESTERN OMELET
D'Shon McCarty, Phoenix, Arizona
(Pictured above)

*The very first time I served this luscious omelet to my hus-
band and young daughters, it became a Yuletide tradition!
Now I always double the savory recipe and sometimes substitute cheddar for Swiss cheese.*

      3 green onions, sliced
  1/2 cup chopped sweet red pepper
      1 tablespoon vegetable oil
      6 eggs, beaten
      1 cup (4 ounces) shredded Swiss cheese
      6 ounces cubed fully cooked ham
  1/3 cup water

In a 10-in. ovenproof skillet, saute the onions and red
pepper in oil for 5 minutes. In a bowl, combine the eggs,
cheese, ham and water. Pour over vegetable mixture. Bake,
uncovered, at 375° for 15-20 minutes or until set. **Yield:** 6
servings.

BREAKFAST ENCHILADA BAKE
Loree Ellis, Colorado Springs, Colorado

*My sister gave me this fuss-free recipe for a hot hearty break-
fast dish, and I can't tell you how many times I've used it for
holiday brunch. I love it because it's full of flavor, fast and filling enough to hold us through Christmas Day.*

      2 cups chopped shaved deli ham
  1/2 cup chopped green onions
  1/2 cup chopped green pepper
      1 package (10 ounces) frozen chopped spinach,
        thawed and squeezed dry
      1 can (4 ounces) chopped green chilies
1-1/4 cups shredded cheddar cheese
1-1/4 cups shredded Monterey Jack cheese
      8 flour tortillas (6 inches)
      6 eggs
2-1/2 cups half-and-half cream
      2 tablespoons all-purpose flour

  1/4 teaspoon garlic powder
  1/4 teaspoon salt
      2 to 3 drops hot pepper sauce

In a large bowl, combine the first five ingredients. In another bowl, combine the cheeses. Spoon about 1/4 cup
of ham mixture off-center on each tortilla; sprinkle with 2
tablespoons cheese mixture. Fold sides and ends over filling and roll up. Place seam side down in a greased 13-in.
x 9-in. x 2-in. baking dish.
   In a bowl, whisk the eggs, cream, flour, garlic powder,
salt and hot pepper sauce. Pour over tortillas. Sprinkle
with the remaining ham mixture. Cover and bake at 350°
for 50 minutes. Uncover; sprinkle with the remaining
cheeses. Bake 5-10 minutes longer or until cheese is melted. **Yield:** 8 servings.

CAJUN SAUSAGE BREAD
Flora Hicks, Collinston, Louisiana

*I found this fun recipe in a newspaper years ago and always
serve it up for special brunches—and for my Super Bowl crowd.
The spicy, stick-to-your-ribs loaf really warms folks up, and
family and friends just rave about it.*

      1 pound bulk spicy pork sausage
      2 to 3 garlic cloves, minced
1-1/2 cups finely chopped green onions
  1/2 cup finely chopped green pepper
      2 jalapeno peppers, seeded and chopped
      3 cups (12 ounces) shredded cheddar cheese
      2 loaves (1 pound *each*) frozen white bread
        dough, thawed
      2 tablespoons butter, melted

Crumble sausage into a large skillet; add garlic. Cook over
medium heat until meat is no longer pink; drain. In a
large bowl, combine the onions, green pepper and jala-
penos. Stir in the sausage mixture and cheese; set aside.
   On a lightly floured surface, roll each loaf of dough into a 13-in. x 9-in. rectangle. Top with sausage mixture to
within 1/2 in. of edges. Roll up jelly-roll style, starting
from a long side; pinch seams to seal. Place seam side down
on greased baking sheets. Brush with butter. Bake at 350°
for 35-40 minutes or until golden brown. Serve warm. Refrigerate leftovers. **Yield:** 2 loaves.
   Editor's Note: When cutting or seeding hot peppers, use
rubber or plastic gloves to protect your hands. Avoid touching your face.

SPICED PEACHES
Patricia Rutherford, Winchester, Illinois

*Here's a pretty dish with old-time sugar 'n' spice flavor that's
a holiday tradition in our family—for brunch or dinner. It's also a wonderfully easy way to put plain old canned peaches in
a festive mood!*

      3 cans (29 ounces *each*) peach halves
Cinnamon sticks (3 inches)
     22 whole cloves
      2 cups sugar
  1/2 cup cider vinegar
      1 teaspoon red food coloring, optional

Drain peaches, reserving 1 cup juice. Set peaches aside. Place cinnamon sticks and cloves on a double thickness of cheesecloth; bring up corners of cloth and tie with string to form a bag. In a saucepan, combine the sugar, vinegar, food coloring if desired and reserved peach juice. Add spice bag. Bring to a boil. Reduce heat; simmer, uncovered, for 10 minutes. Cool slightly.

Place the peaches in a large bowl. Pour sauce over peaches; stir gently to coat. Cover and refrigerate for 2 days, stirring occasionally. Discard spice bag. **Yield:** 22 servings.

SQUASH QUICHE
Candace Miller, Tallahassee, Florida

This is the only quiche my family cares for—and the only way I can ever get them to eat squash! It's chock-full of flavor and fresh veggies, and guests never fail to give it star billing at my holiday brunch.

> 1 unbaked pastry shell (9 inches)
> 2 medium zucchini, peeled and shredded
> 2 medium yellow summer squash, peeled and shredded
> 2 medium carrots, shredded
> 1 medium onion, grated
> 2 tablespoons butter
> 3 eggs, beaten
> 1 cup (4 ounces) shredded Swiss cheese
> 3/4 cup sour cream
> 1/3 cup evaporated milk
> 1/4 teaspoon salt
> 1/4 teaspoon white pepper
> Dash dried thyme

Line unpricked pastry shell with a double thickness of heavy-duty foil. Bake at 450° for 5 minutes; remove foil. Bake 5 minutes longer; set aside. Reduce heat to 350°.

In a large saucepan, cover and cook the zucchini, yellow squash, carrots and onion in butter over low heat for 10-15 minutes or until tender, stirring occasionally. In a small bowl, combine the eggs, cheese, sour cream, milk, salt, pepper and thyme. Spoon vegetable mixture into crust; top with egg mixture.

Bake for 40-45 minutes or until a knife inserted near the center comes out clean. Let stand for 10 minutes before cutting. **Yield:** 6-8 servings.

Breakfast Tips

● During the holiday season, make French toast with eggnog instead of the usual egg and milk mixture. It's a great way to use up extra eggnog, and the French toast really tastes great!

● Turn pancakes as soon as they puff up and fill with bubbles. If you wait for the bubbles to break, the pancakes will be tough.

● If you open a large package of bacon but only use a few slices, place the other pieces in a single layer on a cookie sheet and freeze. Then store frozen slices in a resealable plastic bag; remove, thaw and cook as needed.

OVERNIGHT PECAN FRENCH TOAST
Larry Laatsch, Saginaw, Michigan
(Pictured below)

Whenever our family gathers for Christmas brunch, this convenient make-ahead dish is one crowd-pleaser I can count on. It's a mouth-watering cross between French toast and sticky pecan rolls—and really something to celebrate!

> 8 eggs, lightly beaten
> 1-1/2 cups half-and-half cream
> 2 tablespoons vanilla extract
> 8 to 10 large slices French bread (3/4 inch thick)
> 1 cup packed brown sugar
> 1/2 cup butter, melted
> 1/2 cup maple syrup
> 1/2 cup chopped pecans

In an ungreased 13-in. x 9-in. x 2-in. baking dish, combine the eggs, cream and vanilla. Add bread slices; soak for 5 minutes. Turn bread over; cover and refrigerate overnight.

In a bowl, combine the brown sugar, butter, syrup and pecans. Pour into a greased 13-in. x 9-in. x 2-in. baking dish. Top with bread. Bake, uncovered, at 350° for 30-35 minutes or until lightly browned. **Yield:** 4 servings.

Holiday Breads

Bring back merry mouth-watering memories of Christmases past with the aroma of fresh-baked breads, muffins and rolls warm from the oven.

OLD-FASHIONED DOUGHNUTS
Darlene Markel, Salem, Oregon
(Pictured at left)

These finger-licking-good delicacies are so light and luscious, my family has always referred to them as "Angel Food Doughnuts!" They're lovely at Christmas with a dusting of confectioners' sugar.

> 4 cups all-purpose flour
> 2 teaspoons baking powder
> 1/2 teaspoon baking soda
> 1/4 teaspoon salt
> 1/2 cup sour cream
> 1/2 cup buttermilk
> 1 cup sugar
> 3 eggs
> 1 teaspoon vanilla extract
> Oil for deep-fat frying
> Confectioners' sugar

Combine the flour, baking powder, baking soda and salt; set aside. In a mixing bowl, beat the sour cream and buttermilk until smooth. Add sugar; mix well. Add the eggs and vanilla; mix until combined. Add flour mixture; mix just until combined (dough will be sticky). Cover and refrigerate for 2-3 hours.

Turn dough onto a well-floured surface; knead for 2-3 minutes or until smooth. Roll out to 1/2-in. thickness. Cut with a floured 2-1/2-in. doughnut cutter.

In an electric skillet or deep-fat fryer, heat oil to 375°. Fry doughnuts, a few at a time, for 3 minutes or until golden brown on each side. Fry doughnut holes until golden brown. Drain on paper towels. Dust with confectioners' sugar if desired. **Yield:** about 1-1/2 dozen doughnuts plus doughnut holes.

WALNUT-SWIRL LEMON LOAVES
Theresa Washinski, Wilkes-Barre, Pennsylvania
(Pictured at left)

Here's a rich yeasty loaf, swirled with walnuts, that's a treat any time of year. Drizzled with a light lemony glaze, it also makes a lip-smacking Yuletide gift.

> 2 packages (1/4 ounce *each*) active dry yeast
> 1/2 cup warm water (110° to 115°)
> 1/2 cup warm milk (110° to 115°)
> 1/2 cup sugar
> 1/4 cup vegetable oil
> 2 teaspoons salt
> 1 teaspoon grated lemon peel
> 2 eggs
> 4-1/4 to 4-3/4 cups all-purpose flour
> 1 can (14 ounces) sweetened condensed milk

❄ ❄ ❄

HOME-BAKED HOLIDAY BONANZA includes (from top to bottom, p. 18): yummy treats such as Old-Fashioned Doughnuts, luscious Walnut-Swirl Lemon Loaves and pretty, colorful Christmas Tree Danish.

> 1/3 cup lemon juice
> 1-1/2 cups chopped walnuts
> 2 tablespoons butter, melted
> GLAZE:
> 2-1/3 cups confectioners' sugar
> 2 tablespoons milk
> 1 tablespoon lemon juice

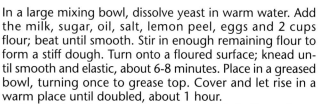

In a large mixing bowl, dissolve yeast in warm water. Add the milk, sugar, oil, salt, lemon peel, eggs and 2 cups flour; beat until smooth. Stir in enough remaining flour to form a stiff dough. Turn onto a floured surface; knead until smooth and elastic, about 6-8 minutes. Place in a greased bowl, turning once to grease top. Cover and let rise in a warm place until doubled, about 1 hour.

Punch dough down. Turn onto a lightly floured surface; divide in thirds. Roll each portion into a 13-in. x 12-in. rectangle. Combine condensed milk and lemon juice until blended; spread over dough to within 1/2 in. of edges. Sprinkle with walnuts. Roll up jelly-roll style, starting with a long side; pinch seams to seal and tuck ends under. Place seam side down on greased baking sheets. Cover and let rise in a warm place until doubled, about 40 minutes.

Bake at 350° for 30-35 minutes or until golden brown. Remove from pans to wire racks; brush with butter. Cool completely. For glaze, combine confectioners' sugar and milk until smooth; stir in lemon juice. Drizzle over bread. **Yield:** 3 loaves.

CHRISTMAS TREE DANISH
Julia Byers, Rensselaer, New York
(Pictured at left)

I've been making these tender mini trees for nearly 40 years— and folks still keep asking for them! With almond filling, maraschino cherry "ornaments" and iced garlands, the flaky pastries taste as festive as they look.

> 4-3/4 cups all-purpose flour, *divided*
> 1 cup cold butter
> 3-1/4 teaspoons active dry yeast
> 1-1/4 cups warm milk (110° to 115°)
> 1 egg, beaten
> 1/4 cup sugar
> 1 teaspoon salt
> ALMOND FILLING:
> 4 ounces almond paste
> 1/2 cup sugar
> 1 egg
> 1 egg yolk, beaten
> 14 green candied cherries, quartered
> 14 red candied cherries, quartered
> ICING:
> 1-1/2 cups confectioners' sugar
> 2 tablespoons water
> 1/2 teaspoon almond extract

Sprinkle 1 tablespoon flour over a work surface; place butter on surface and sprinkle with 1 teaspoon flour. Press and roll out with a rolling pin. Scrape butter from rolling pin and continue to work the butter until it forms a smooth mass without any hard lumps. Knead in 1/4 cup flour, working quickly to keep butter cold.

Place butter mixture on a sheet of plastic wrap and shape into a small rectangle. Cover with another sheet of plastic wrap; roll into a 9-in. x 6-in. rectangle. Wrap in plastic wrap and refrigerate.

In a large mixing bowl, dissolve yeast in warm milk. Add egg, sugar and salt; beat until smooth. Stir in the remaining flour to form a soft dough. Turn onto a floured surface; cover and let rest for 5 minutes. Roll into a 14-in. x 10-in. rectangle, with the short side toward the bottom. Unwrap butter mixture; position on dough 1 in. above bottom edge and 1/2 in. from each side edge. Fold top half of dough over butter and pinch edges to seal.

Turn dough a quarter turn to the right; sprinkle lightly with additional flour. Lightly roll into a 16-in. x 8-in. rectangle. Fold bottom third of rectangle up and top third down, as when folding a business letter, making a 5-1/2-in. x 8-in. rectangle (this is called one turn). Rotate dough a quarter turn to the right. Lightly roll into a 16-in. x 8-in. rectangle and again fold into thirds, finishing the second turn. Repeat rotating, rolling and folding two more times for a total of four turns. (If at any time the butter gets soft, refrigerate for 10-15 minutes.) Wrap in plastic wrap; refrigerate for 30 minutes.

For filling, in a mixing bowl, beat the almond paste, sugar and egg until smooth; set aside. Roll dough into a 22-in. x 7-in. rectangle. Cut lengthwise into fourteen 1/2-in. strips. Twist each strip and form into a tree shape by zigzagging dough on ungreased baking sheets. Brush with egg yolk. Dot with filling. Decorate with cherries. Let rise in a warm place until doubled, about 20 minutes.

Bake at 350° for 15-20 minutes or until golden brown. Cool on wire racks. Combine the icing ingredients; drizzle over trees. **Yield:** 14 servings.

CROISSANTS
Dorothy Southard, Cato, New York

These flaky, light golden-brown croissants will make holiday lunch or dinner something special for your family—and the overnight dough will make things more convenient for you!

6-1/4 to 7 cups all-purpose flour
  1/2 cup sugar
    1 package (1/4 ounce) active dry yeast
1-1/2 teaspoons salt
    2 cups plus 1 tablespoon milk, *divided*
  1/4 cup water
    1 cup cold butter, cubed
    1 egg

In a large mixing bowl, combine 3 cups flour, sugar, yeast and salt. In a saucepan, heat 2 cups milk and water to 120°-130°. Add to dry ingredients; beat on medium speed for 2 minutes. Stir in enough remaining flour to form a soft dough.

Turn onto a floured surface; knead until smooth and elastic, about 6-8 minutes. Place in a greased bowl, turning once to grease top. Cover and let rise in a warm place until doubled, about 1-1/4 hours.

Meanwhile, in a small mixing bowl, beat butter until softened but still cold. Spread half of the butter into a 10-in. x 9-in. rectangle on a piece of waxed paper. Cover with

waxed paper and refrigerate. Repeat with remaining butter.

Punch dough down. Turn onto a lightly floured surface; divide dough into two pieces. Roll one piece into a 15-in. x 10-in. rectangle. Remove top sheet from butter; invert over two-thirds of dough. Remove other sheet. Fold unbuttered dough over butter. Fold other side over top. Roll out into a 15-in. x 10-in. rectangle. Fold into thirds. Repeat rolling and folding twice. Wrap in plastic wrap; refrigerate at least 2 hours or overnight. Repeat with remaining dough and butter.

On a floured surface, roll one piece into a 25-in. x 5-in. rectangle. Cut into 5-in. squares. Cut each square diagonally in half, forming two triangles. Roll up triangles from the wide end and place point side down 2 in. apart on ungreased baking sheets. Curve ends down to form crescent shape. Repeat with remaining dough. Cover and let rise until doubled, about 40 minutes.

In a small bowl, beat egg with remaining milk. Brush over rolls. Bake at 400° for 14-18 minutes or until golden brown. Remove with a spatula to wire racks to cool. **Yield:** 20 rolls.

DUTCH OAT BREAD
Joan Meindertsma, Laguna Niguel, California

This delicious healthful bread is packed with oats and bran, tastes great toasted and is so easy that I always bake extra loaves for gifts. The recipe is from a 95-year-old friend who brought it from Holland.

  1 cup all-purpose flour
  1 cup old-fashioned oats
  1 cup All-Bran
2/3 cup sugar
  1 teaspoon baking soda
1/2 teaspoon salt
  1 egg, beaten
  1 cup buttermilk
  1 teaspoon sour cream

In a large bowl, combine the dry ingredients. In a small bowl, combine the egg, buttermilk and sour cream; mix well. Stir into the dry ingredients just until moistened.

Pour into a greased 8-in. x 4-in. x 2-in. loaf pan. Bake at 350° for 42-47 minutes or until a toothpick inserted near the center comes out clean. Cool for 10 minutes before removing from pan to a wire rack. **Yield:** 1 loaf.

RAISIN BRAN MUFFINS
Rosemary McGuire, Anderson, Indiana

Who'd believe that muffins this tender and tasty could be so quick and easy to make? The cereal adds a touch of sweetness and crunch. These are so nice to have on hand!

  1 package (15 ounces) Raisin Bran
  5 cups all-purpose flour
  3 cups sugar
  5 teaspoons baking soda
  2 teaspoons salt
  4 eggs, beaten
  4 cups buttermilk
  1 cup vegetable oil

In a large bowl, combine the dry ingredients. Combine

the eggs, buttermilk and oil; stir into dry ingredients just until moistened.

Fill greased or paper-lined muffin cups two-thirds full. Bake at 400° for 12-16 minutes or until a toothpick comes out clean. Cool for 5 minutes before removing from pans to wire racks. **Yield:** 3-1/2 dozen.

HAZELNUT YEAST BREAD
Ruth Burris, Zionsville, Indiana

A flurry of Yuletide activities—and a tasty recipe—can help you make the most of your handy bread machine during this hectic time. This hearty loaf is nutty and simply delicious.

```
2/3 cup warm milk (70° to 80°)
  2 tablespoons butter, melted
  1 egg
1/2 teaspoon almond extract
1/2 teaspoon salt
  2 cups bread flour
  2 tablespoons sugar
  1 package (1/4 ounce) active dry yeast
1/2 cup chopped hazelnuts, toasted
```

In bread machine pan, place the first eight ingredients in order suggested by manufacturer. Select basic bread setting. Choose crust color and loaf size if available. Bake according to bread machine directions (check dough after 5 minutes of mixing; add 1 to 2 tablespoons of water or flour if needed).

Just before the final kneading (your bread machine may audibly signal this), add the hazelnuts. **Yield:** 1 loaf (1 pound).

Editor's Note: If your bread machine has a time-delay feature, we recommend you do not use it for this recipe.

APRICOT KOLACHES
Arlyn Kramer, Dumas, Arkansas

Pastries as pretty as these make any gathering special. I like to bake them a day in advance because they do take some time to prepare—but guests agree they're worth it!

```
7-3/4 to 8-1/4 cups all-purpose flour
    2/3 cup sugar
      1 tablespoon active dry yeast
      2 teaspoons salt
  2-1/2 cups milk
      1 cup plus 2 tablespoons butter, cubed, divided
      4 egg yolks
      2 cans (12 ounces each) apricot filling
GLAZE:
    3/4 cup confectioners' sugar
      1 to 2 tablespoons water
```

In a large mixing bowl, combine 2 cups flour, sugar, yeast and salt. In a saucepan, heat milk and 1 cup butter to 120°-130°. Add to dry ingredients; beat until moistened. Add egg yolks; beat on low speed for 30 seconds. Beat on high for 3 minutes. Stir in enough remaining flour to form a soft dough.

Turn onto a floured surface; knead until smooth and elastic, about 6-8 minutes. Place in a greased bowl, turning once to grease top. Cover and let rise in a warm place until doubled, about 1 hour.

Punch dough down. Turn onto a lightly floured surface. Shape into 1-1/2-in. balls; roll each into a 2-1/2-in. circle. Place 2 in. apart on greased baking sheets. Cover and let rise until doubled, about 30 minutes.

Using the end of a wooden spoon, make a 1-1/2-in. indentation in the center of each roll; fill with about 2 teaspoons apricot filling. Melt remaining butter; brush over dough. Bake at 350° for 15-20 minutes or until golden brown. Remove from pans to wire racks to cool. Combine glaze ingredients; drizzle over rolls. **Yield:** about 4 dozen.

Editor's Note: This recipe was tested with Solo filling.

CRANBERRY LEMON BREAD
Joan Wilson, Galesburg, Illinois
(Pictured above)

Laced with lemon flavor and studded with tangy cranberries, this quick bread is an old family favorite.

```
    2/3 cup shortening
1-2/3 cups sugar
      3 eggs
    1/2 cup sour cream
1-1/4 teaspoons lemon extract
2-1/3 cups all-purpose flour
1-1/4 teaspoons baking powder
1-1/4 teaspoons baking soda
      1 teaspoon salt
      1 cup buttermilk
1-1/4 cups dried cranberries
      2 teaspoons poppy seeds, optional
```

In a large mixing bowl, cream shortening and sugar. Add eggs, one at a time, beating well after each addition. Add sour cream and lemon extract; mix well. Combine the flour, baking powder, baking soda and salt; add to creamed mixture alternately with buttermilk. Fold in cranberries and poppy seeds if desired.

Pour into four greased 5-3/4-in. x 3-in. x 2-in. loaf pans. Bake at 350° for 40-50 minutes or until a toothpick comes out clean. Cool for 10 minutes before removing from pans to wire racks. **Yield:** 4 mini loaves.

Appealing Appetizers

Warm up any Yuletide gathering with a flurry of fun finger foods, hearty hors d'oeuvres and savory snacks by the sleighful.

ZIPPY PARTY ROLL-UPS
Donna Gonzalez del Valle, Battle Ground, Washington
(Pictured at left)

A guaranteed Christmas crowd-pleaser, these zesty appetizers are a great way to pep up a party! The recipe won a blue ribbon at the county fair, and even though I always double it, I never seem to make enough.

    1 package (8 ounces) cream cheese, softened
    6 flour tortillas (8 inches)
    36 fresh spinach leaves
    1 package (6 ounces) thinly sliced deli ham
    1 can (4 ounces) chopped green chilies, drained
    1 can (2-1/4 ounces) chopped ripe olives, drained

Spread about 3 tablespoons of cream cheese over each tortilla; layer each with six spinach leaves and three slices of ham. Sprinkle with chilies and olives. Roll up tightly and wrap in plastic wrap. Refrigerate until firm. Unwrap and cut into slices. **Yield:** about 4 dozen.

MINI BACON QUICHES
Julie Nowakowski, LaSalle, Illinois
(Pictured at left)

Bite-size and brimming with bacon and cheese, these melt-in-your-mouth tidbits are easy for guests to handle, and they look so colorful on a buffet. Nobody can stop with just one.

    1 package (15 ounces) refrigerated pie pastry
    1/2 pound sliced bacon, cooked and crumbled
    1/2 cup ricotta cheese
    1/2 cup shredded cheddar cheese
    1/2 cup shredded mozzarella cheese
    1 egg, lightly beaten
    1 small onion, finely chopped
    1/4 teaspoon garlic powder
    1/8 teaspoon salt
Dash pepper
Dash cayenne pepper
    2 teaspoons all-purpose flour

Let pastry stand at room temperature for 15-20 minutes. In a bowl, combine the bacon, cheeses, egg, onion, garlic powder, salt, pepper and cayenne. Sprinkle each pastry crust with 1 teaspoon flour; place floured side down on a lightly floured surface. Cut 12 circles from each crust, using a 2-1/2-in. round biscuit cutter.

Press dough onto the bottom and up the sides of lightly greased miniature muffin cups. Fill each with about 1 tablespoon of bacon mixture. Bake at 400° for 16-18 minutes or until filling is set. Cool for 5 minutes before removing from pans to a wire rack. Serve warm. **Yield:** 2 dozen.

❄ ❄ ❄

TEMPTING TASTE-TEASERS. Jump-start your holiday parties with these scrumptious munchies (top to bottom, p. 22): Zippy Party Roll-Ups, flavorful Flying Chicken Wings and bite-size Mini Bacon Quiches.

FLYING CHICKEN WINGS
Shirley Dee McMurtry, Dolliver, Iowa
(Pictured at left)

These golden wings are finger-licking favorites at every festive family get-together. Delicious hot or cold, they're easy to make, and they "fly" off the plate whenever I serve them!

    20 whole chicken wings (about 4 pounds)
    1 cup soy sauce
    1 cup sugar
    1/4 cup pineapple juice
    1/4 cup vegetable oil
    1 teaspoon garlic salt
    1 teaspoon ground ginger

Cut chicken wings into three sections; discard wing tip portion. In a large resealable plastic bag, combine the remaining ingredients; add chicken wings. Seal bag and turn to coat; refrigerate overnight.

Drain and discard marinade. Place the wings in a greased 15-in. x 10-in. x 1-in. baking pan. Bake, uncovered, at 350° for 1 hour or until juices run clear, turning once. **Yield:** 16 servings.

Editor's Note: 4 pounds of uncooked chicken wing sections (wingettes) may be substituted for the whole chicken wings. Omit the first step in the recipe.

GUACAMOLE STUFFED EGGS
Phy Bresse, Lumberton, North Carolina

Looking for a quick and easy way to wish guests "Feliz Navidad?" Try my flavorful south-of-the-border variation on deviled eggs. Guests say they're heavenly.

    6 hard-cooked eggs
    1/4 cup guacamole dip
    1 teaspoon lime juice
    1 tablespoon minced fresh cilantro
    1/4 teaspoon salt, optional
Paprika, optional

Cut eggs in half lengthwise; remove yolks and set whites aside. In a small bowl, mash yolks with a fork. Stir in the guacamole, lime juice, cilantro and salt if desired. Spoon or pipe into egg whites. Sprinkle with paprika if desired. Refrigerate until serving. **Yield:** 1 dozen.

Appetizer Tips

● Always allow cheese balls or dips and spreads that contain cream cheese to stand at room temperature 15 minutes before serving for more flavor and easier spreading.

● To make deviled eggs sit flat on a plate, slice a tiny piece from the bottom of each half.

KIELBASA BUTTONS WITH SPICY APRICOT SAUCE
Norma Phillips, Worcester, Massachusetts

Welcome guests in from the cold with these spicy glazed sausage bites served with pretty party picks. They couldn't be easier to make, and people just gobble them up!

- 1 pound fully cooked kielbasa *or* Polish sausage, cut into 1/4-inch slices
- 1/4 cup apricot preserves
- 1/4 cup barbecue sauce
- 1/8 teaspoon crushed red pepper flakes
- 5 drops hot pepper sauce

In a large skillet, brown sausage slices on both sides; drain on paper towels. In the same skillet, combine the preserves, barbecue sauce, pepper flakes and hot pepper sauce. Return sausage to the pan; cook and stir over medium heat for 3-5 minutes or until heated through. Serve with toothpicks. **Yield:** about 3-1/2 cups.

CHEESE 'N' HAM BISCUIT DROPS
Mary Detweiler, West Farmington, Ohio

Flecked with golden cheddar and ham, these flavorful party puffs disappear in two bites. Lucky for you, the recipe is sized to feed a hungry crowd.

- 4 cups (16 ounces) shredded cheddar cheese
- 3 cups biscuit/baking mix
- 1-1/2 cups finely chopped fully cooked ham (about 10 ounces)
- 1/2 cup grated Parmesan cheese
- 2 tablespoons minced fresh parsley
- 2/3 cup milk
- 2 teaspoons spicy brown mustard

In a large bowl, combine all ingredients; mix well. Shape into 1-in. balls. Place 1 in. apart on greased baking sheets. Bake at 350° for 20-25 minutes or until lightly browned. Serve warm. **Yield:** 7 dozen.

BRAUNSCHWEIGER SNOWBALL
Pat Gulley, Harrisburg, Illinois

Even folks who normally don't care for braunschweiger can't seem to resist this creamy spread. Topped with red and green peppers, it's a natural for holiday entertaining. Sometimes I like to form a "wreath" of fresh parsley around it.

- 1 pound braunschweiger
- 1 package (8 ounces) cream cheese, softened
- 1/2 cup chili sauce
- 1 tablespoon chopped onion
- 1 teaspoon Worcestershire sauce
- 1 teaspoon prepared horseradish, optional

TOPPING:
- 1 package (3 ounces) cream cheese, softened
- 1/4 cup mayonnaise
- 2 tablespoons finely chopped sweet red *and/or* green pepper

Assorted crackers

In a large mixing bowl, combine the first six ingredients; beat until blended. Place on a large sheet of plastic wrap; using plastic wrap, shape mixture into a large ball. Transfer to a serving plate; refrigerate.

For topping, in a small mixing bowl, beat the cream cheese and mayonnaise until smooth. Remove plastic wrap from braunschweiger ball; spread with topping. Sprinkle with chopped pepper. Serve with crackers. **Yield:** 1 ball (5 cups).

CHILI CHEESE BALL
Sandy Wagner, Fond du Lac, Wisconsin

It wouldn't be Christmas at our house without this zippy, well-seasoned cheese ball—my husband's absolute favorite. The family starts asking about it 2 weeks before the holidays! It's also a big hit at Super Bowl parties.

- 1 package (8 ounces) cream cheese, softened
- 1-1/2 cups (6 ounces) shredded Monterey Jack cheese
- 1 piece (4 ounces) Gouda cheese, shredded
- 1 can (4-1/4 ounces) chopped ripe olives, drained
- 2 tablespoons dried minced onion
- 1 tablespoon prepared mustard
- 3-1/2 teaspoons chili powder, *divided*
- 1/2 teaspoon garlic powder
- 1/2 cup chopped almonds, toasted

Assorted crackers

In a mixing bowl, beat cream cheese until fluffy. Add the Monterey Jack and Gouda; mix well. Stir in the olives, onion and mustard. Add 2 teaspoons chili powder and the garlic powder. Shape into a ball. Combine almonds and remaining chili powder; roll cheese ball in almond mixture. Wrap tightly in plastic wrap. Refrigerate for several hours or overnight. Serve with crackers. **Yield:** 1 cheese ball (2-1/2 cups).

CINNAMON-SUGAR WALNUTS
Brenda Osborne, Cleveland, Tennessee

You can never have too many merry munchies for drop-in visitors and Christmas get-togethers. And Santa himself could not resist a mitten-full of these sweet walnut treats.

- 3 cups walnut halves
- 1 cup sugar
- 1/2 cup strong brewed coffee
- 1 to 1-1/2 teaspoons ground cinnamon
- 1/2 teaspoon salt
- 1 teaspoon vanilla extract

Spread walnuts in a single layer on a baking sheet. Bake at 350° for 5 minutes or until warmed. Cover and keep warm. In a large heavy saucepan, combine the sugar, coffee, cinnamon and salt. Bring to a boil over medium heat. Cook, without stirring, until a candy thermometer reads 250° (hard-ball stage).

Remove from the heat; stir in vanilla. Add walnuts; toss to coat. Pour into a greased 15-in. x 10-in. x 1-in. baking pan; separate with a fork. Cool. Store in an airtight container in the refrigerator. **Yield:** 4 cups.

Editor's Note: We recommend that you test your candy thermometer before each use by bringing water to a boil; the thermometer should read 212°. Adjust your recipe temperature up or down based on your test.

CHEERY CRANBERRY NOG
Nella Parker, Hersey, Michigan
(Pictured above)

Tangy cranberry flavors this frothy foamy beverage that's as refreshing as a yogurt smoothie. It always brings a blush of Christmas to my holiday spreads…and lots of compliments from guests of all ages.

2 cups half-and-half cream
6 eggs
1 cup sugar
3 cups heavy whipping cream
2 cans (11-1/2 ounces *each*) cranberry juice
    oncentrate, undiluted
2 cups water

In a Dutch oven, combine the half-and-half, eggs and sugar. Cook and stir over medium-low heat until mixture reaches 160° and coats the back of a metal spoon. Remove from the heat; cool slightly. Stir in the remaining ingredients. Cover and refrigerate until chilled. **Yield:** 3 quarts.

PICKLED MUSHROOMS
Joyce Anderson, Chico, California

I'm always asked to bring these tempting tidbits to holiday gatherings. Easy to make ahead and transport, they're something to celebrate on a festive relish tray.

2/3 cup white wine vinegar
1/2 cup vegetable oil
2 tablespoons water
1 teaspoon salt
Dash pepper
Dash hot pepper sauce
1 pound small whole fresh mushrooms
1 medium onion, thinly sliced
2 to 4 garlic cloves, thinly sliced

In a large glass jar with a tight-fitting lid, combine the first six ingredients. Add the mushrooms, onion and garlic. Cover and shake gently to coat. Refrigerate for 8 hours or overnight. Drain before serving. **Yield:** 4-1/2 cups.

CORDON BLEU EGG ROLLS
Kit Shaw, Boise, Idaho

These delicious golden egg rolls disappear at parties…but my kids love them all year-round. I often freeze a batch and let them microwave a couple for after-school snacks.

1/2 pound frozen breaded chicken tenders, thawed
    and cubed
1-1/2 cups cubed cooked chicken
1 cup (4 ounces) shredded Swiss cheese
1/3 pound cubed deli ham
1/2 cup honey mustard
1/4 cup sliced ripe olives, drained
24 egg roll wrappers
Canola oil for frying
DIPPING SAUCE:
1/2 cup mayonnaise
3 tablespoons honey mustard

In a large bowl, combine the first six ingredients. Place about 1/4 cupful in the center of each egg roll wrapper. Fold bottom corner over filling; fold sides toward center over filling. Moisten remaining corner with water; roll up tightly to seal.

In an electric skillet, heat 1 in. of oil to 375°. Fry egg rolls, a few at a time, for 1-2 minutes on each side or until golden brown. Drain on paper towels. In a small bowl, combine the sauce ingredients. Serve with egg rolls. **Yield:** 2 dozen.

ZESTY MEATBALLS
Debbie Segate, Grande Prairie, Alberta

Orange juice lends wonderful tang to these tender tasty meatballs. They're one of my most popular appetizers, and I can make them ahead, then pop in the oven an hour before serving. A do-ahead delight during this busy season!

1 egg white, beaten
3/4 cup graham cracker crumbs (about 12 squares)
3 tablespoons milk
2 teaspoons prepared mustard
1/4 teaspoon salt
3/4 pound lean ground beef
3/4 pound ground turkey
SAUCE:
1 cup barbecue sauce
1 can (6 ounces) frozen orange juice concentrate,
    thawed
1/4 cup water

In a bowl, combine the egg white, cracker crumbs, milk, mustard and salt. Crumble beef and turkey over mixture and mix well. Shape into 1-1/2-in. balls. Place in a lightly greased 15-in. x 10-in. x 1-in. baking pan. Bake at 375° for 20 minutes or until meat is no longer pink.

Transfer meatballs to a greased 2-qt. baking dish. Combine sauce ingredients; pour over meatballs. Cover and bake at 350° for 1 hour. **Yield:** 3 dozen.

MISTLETOE MENU. Rich recipes are (clockwise from lower left): Spiced Roast Goose (p. 28), Holiday Spice Cheesecake (p. 29), Mustard Green Beans (p. 28), Apricot Almond Dressing (p. 28) and Christmas Cranberry Salad (p. 28).

Celebrate the spirit of the season with loved ones gathered near and a festive meal rich in tradition, warmth and good cheer!

SPICED ROAST GOOSE
Iola Egle, Bella Vista, Arkansas
(Pictured on page 26)

As pretty as a picture with its caramelized seasoning rub, this festive goose is guaranteed to be a holiday showstopper! Best of all, it tastes as delicious as it looks and fills the house with an incredible aroma as it cooks.

    4 cups water, *divided*
    2/3 cup plus 1 tablespoon soy sauce, *divided*
    1/4 cup chopped celery
    1/4 cup dried minced onion
    1 tablespoon sugar
    1 domestic goose (10 to 12 pounds)
Salt and pepper
    2 teaspoons ground cinnamon
    1 teaspoon garlic powder
    1 teaspoon aniseed
    1/4 cup cider vinegar
    1/4 cup honey
    2 teaspoons cornstarch
    2 tablespoons cold water

In a large saucepan, combine 2 cups water, 2/3 cup soy sauce, celery, onion and sugar. Bring to a boil. Reduce heat; cook, uncovered, until vegetables are tender, stirring frequently. Cool. Pour marinade into a large resealable plastic bag; add goose. Seal bag and turn to coat; refrigerate for 3-4 hours, turning several times.

Drain and discard marinade. Sprinkle goose cavity with salt and pepper. Place on a rack in a shallow roasting pan. Combine the cinnamon, garlic powder and aniseed; rub over goose. Bake, uncovered, at 325° for 30 minutes.

Meanwhile, in a small saucepan, combine the vinegar, honey and remaining water and soy sauce. Bring to a boil. Reduce heat; simmer, uncovered, until reduced by about half. Baste goose with honey mixture. Bake, uncovered, for 30 minutes. Cover and bake 1-1/2 to 2 hours longer or until a meat thermometer reads 180°, basting occasionally with remaining honey mixture if desired. Cover and let stand for 15 minutes before carving.

For gravy, strain pan juices; skim and discard fat. In a small saucepan, combine cornstarch and cold water until smooth. Stir in pan juices. Bring to a boil; cook and stir for 2 minutes or until thickened. Serve with goose. **Yield:** 6-8 servings.

APRICOT ALMOND DRESSING
Kitty Shelton, Ketchum, Idaho
(Pictured on page 27)

Talk about versatile! This light fluffy stuffing goes with almost any entree. The apricots and slivered almonds add a sweet nutty flavor—but if I'm serving it with turkey, I often substitute cranberries and chestnuts.

    2 cups chopped onions
    2 cups chopped celery
    1/2 cup slivered almonds

    1/2 cup butter
    1 can (14-1/2 ounces) chicken broth
    1 package (12 ounces) unseasoned stuffing cubes
    1/4 cup chopped dried apricots
    1 teaspoon *each* rubbed sage, dried thyme and dried rosemary, crushed
Salt and pepper to taste

In a large skillet, saute the onions, celery and almonds in butter until vegetables are tender. Stir in the remaining ingredients. Spoon into a greased 3-qt. baking dish. Cover and bake at 350° for 30 minutes. Uncover; bake 5-10 minutes longer or until heated through. **Yield:** 10 servings.

MUSTARD GREEN BEANS
Mary Graham, Barneveld, Wisconsin
(Pictured on page 27)

Looking for an easy way to dress up veggies in a twinkling? My mother came up with this mouth-watering, family-favorite recipe that we still celebrate at holiday get-together meals!

    3 pounds fresh green beans
    2 tablespoons sugar
    1 tablespoon cornstarch
    1/2 cup cider vinegar
    2 tablespoons water
1-1/2 teaspoons prepared mustard
Dash salt
    1 tablespoon butter

Place beans in a Dutch oven and cover with water; bring to a boil. Cook, uncovered, for 8-10 minutes or until crisp-tender; drain and set aside.

In a small bowl, combine the sugar, cornstarch, vinegar, water, mustard and salt until smooth. In the Dutch oven, melt butter over medium heat. Stir in the mustard mixture. Bring to a boil; cook and stir for 1-2 minutes or until thickened. Return beans to the pan; heat through. **Yield:** 12 servings.

CHRISTMAS CRANBERRY SALAD
Edie DeSpain, Logan, Utah
(Pictured on page 27)

You might find that this yummy gelatin salad is one side dish pretty enough to steal top billing! It's cool, crunchy and refreshing and adds a splash of Christmas color to any table. Garnish with lettuce, orange slices and sugared cranberries.

1-1/2 cups finely chopped fresh *or* frozen cranberries
    1/2 cup sugar
    2 packages (3 ounces *each*) orange *or* lemon gelatin
    1/4 teaspoon salt
    2 cups boiling water
1-1/2 cups cold water
    1 tablespoon lemon juice

1/4 teaspoon ground cinnamon
1/8 teaspoon ground cloves
1 medium navel orange, peeled and diced
1/2 cup chopped almonds
Lettuce leaves

In a small bowl, combine cranberries and sugar; set aside. In a large bowl, dissolve gelatin and salt in boiling water. Stir in the cold water, lemon juice, cinnamon and cloves. Cover and chill for 1 hour.

Stir in the orange, almonds and cranberry mixture. Pour into a 6-cup ring mold coated with nonstick cooking spray. Cover and refrigerate for 3-4 hours or until set. Invert onto a lettuce-lined serving plate. **Yield:** 12 servings.

HOLIDAY SPICE CHEESECAKE
Colleen Arnold, Sublette, Illinois
(Pictured on page 26)

Here is THE perfect dessert to top off Christmas dinner. It's simply stunning with a filling that's creamy and rich with brown sugar, cinnamon and allspice. It freezes well, so busy holiday cooks can make it a month in advance, then defrost in the fridge and trim with whipped cream before serving.

9 whole graham crackers (about 5 inches x 2-1/2 inches)
3/4 cup chopped walnuts
1/4 cup butter, melted
1/2 teaspoon ground cinnamon
FILLING:
3 packages (8 ounces *each*) cream cheese, softened
3/4 cup sugar
3/4 cup packed brown sugar
2-1/4 teaspoons vanilla extract
2 teaspoons ground cinnamon
3/4 teaspoon ground allspice
1/2 teaspoon salt
4 eggs, lightly beaten
2 cups (16 ounces) sour cream
TOPPING:
1 cup heavy whipping cream
2 tablespoons confectioners' sugar
1/4 teaspoon ground cinnamon

Place graham crackers and walnuts in a food processor; cover and process until nuts are finely chopped. Add butter and cinnamon; process until blended. Press onto the bottom and 2 in. up the sides of a greased 9-in. springform pan; set aside.

For filling, in a mixing bowl, beat cream cheese, sugars, vanilla, cinnamon, allspice and salt until smooth. Add eggs; beat on low speed just until combined. Add sour cream; beat on low speed just until combined. Pour into crust. Place pan on a baking sheet. Bake at 350° for 55-65 minutes or until center is almost set. Cool on a wire rack for 10 minutes. Carefully run a knife around edge of pan to loosen; cool 1 hour longer. Refrigerate overnight.

Remove sides of pan. For topping, in a small mixing bowl, beat cream until it begins to thicken. Add confectioners' sugar; beat until soft peaks form. Transfer to a pastry bag with a star tip. Pipe around edge of cheesecake; sprinkle with cinnamon. **Yield:** 12-16 servings.

PORK TENDERLOIN WITH PLUM SAUCE
Doris Chamberlain, South Weymouth, Massachusetts
(Pictured above)

A pretty alternative for a special dinner during the holidays...or any time at all, this pork tenderloin is so tasty and appealing. It's great for warming up guests on cold winter nights and never fails to get raves.

1/2 cup apple cider *or* juice
1/2 cup soy sauce
2 garlic cloves, minced
1 tablespoon ground mustard
1 teaspoon dried thyme
1 teaspoon ground ginger
2 pork tenderloins (about 1 pound *each*)
PLUM SAUCE:
1/2 cup plum preserves
1/4 cup finely chopped onion
1/4 cup apricot preserves
2 tablespoons brown sugar
2 tablespoons apple cider *or* juice
2 tablespoons soy sauce
2 tablespoons ketchup
1 garlic clove, minced

In a small bowl, combine the first six ingredients. Pour 3/4 cup into a large resealable plastic bag; add the pork. Seal bag and turn to coat; refrigerate for at least 2 hours. Cover and refrigerate remaining marinade for basting.

Drain and discard marinade from pork. Place tenderloins on a rack in a shallow roasting pan. Bake, uncovered, at 425° for 40-45 minutes or until a meat thermometer reads 160°, basting twice with reserved marinade.

In a small saucepan, combine sauce ingredients. Bring to a boil. Reduce heat; simmer, uncovered, for 10 minutes or until flavors blend. Let pork stand for 5 minutes before slicing. Serve with plum sauce. **Yield:** 8 servings.

CHOCOLATE MINT CAKE ROLL
Ron Poole, Saluda, North Carolina
(Pictured below)

Folks will "ooh" and "aah" when you set this fancy dessert on the table! It looks like an old-time Yule log, has a minty whipped-cream filling, and is slathered in fudgy frosting topped with chocolate curls. An awesome finale!

3 eggs, *separated*
1 cup sugar, *divided*
2 tablespoons water
1/2 teaspoon vanilla extract
1 cup cake flour
1/4 cup baking cocoa
1 teaspoon baking powder
1/4 teaspoon salt
FILLING:
1-1/2 cups heavy whipping cream
3 tablespoons confectioners' sugar
1/4 teaspoon peppermint extract
3 drops green food coloring
1/3 cup miniature semisweet chocolate chips
FROSTING:
1/4 cup butter, softened
2 cups confectioners' sugar
3 tablespoons baking cocoa
3 tablespoons milk
1/2 teaspoon peppermint extract
1/2 teaspoon vanilla extract
Chocolate curls

In a large mixing bowl, beat egg yolks until slightly thickened. Gradually add 3/4 cup sugar, beating until thick and lemon-colored. Beat in water and vanilla. Combine the flour, cocoa, baking powder and salt; gradually add to yolk mixture and mix well. In another large mixing bowl, beat egg whites until soft peaks form. Add remaining sugar, 1 tablespoon at a time, beating until stiff peaks form. Gradually fold into batter.

Line a greased 15-in. x 10-in. x 1-in. baking pan with waxed paper. Spread batter evenly in pan. Bake at 375° for 10-15 minutes or until cake springs back when lightly touched. Cool for 5 minutes. Invert cake onto a kitchen towel dusted with confectioners' sugar. Gently peel off waxed paper. Roll up cake in the towel, jelly-roll style, starting with a short side. Cool on a wire rack.

For filling, in a small mixing bowl, beat the cream, confectioners' sugar, extract and food coloring until stiff peaks form. Fold in chocolate chips. Unroll cake; spread filling to within 1/2 in. of edges. Roll up again. Place seam side down on a serving platter.

For frosting, in a small mixing bowl, cream butter, confectioners' sugar, cocoa, milk and extracts. Frost cake roll. Refrigerate until serving. Decorate with chocolate curls. **Yield:** 12 servings.

CHICKEN BROCCOLI MANICOTTI
Dennis Willert, Davenport, Iowa

Here's a tasty new way to use up leftover poultry after the holidays. It's a long-standing favorite at our house.

12 uncooked manicotti shells
1 small onion, chopped
3 tablespoons butter
3 tablespoons all-purpose flour
1/4 teaspoon salt
1 cup half-and-half cream
1 cup chicken broth
1-1/2 cups (6 ounces) shredded Monterey Jack cheese
1/4 cup shredded Parmesan cheese
FILLING:
2 eggs, lightly beaten
3/4 cup soft bread crumbs
1/4 cup minced fresh parsley
1/4 teaspoon salt
1/4 teaspoon crushed red pepper flakes
1/8 teaspoon ground nutmeg
4 cups cubed cooked chicken
2 packages (10 ounces *each*) frozen chopped broccoli, thawed

Cook manicotti shells according to package directions. Meanwhile, for sauce, in a large saucepan, saute onion in butter. Stir in flour and salt until blended. Gradually whisk in cream and broth. Bring to a boil; cook and stir for 1-2 minutes or until thickened. Reduce heat; stir in cheeses just until melted.

In a bowl, combine the eggs, bread crumbs, parsley, salt, pepper flakes and nutmeg. Stir in chicken and broccoli. Add 1 cup sauce. Drain shells; stuff with chicken mixture.

Spread about 1/2 cup sauce in two greased 11-in. x 7-in. x 2-in. baking dishes. Place stuffed shells over sauce; top with remaining sauce. Cover and bake at 350° for 35-40 minutes. Uncover; bake 5 minutes longer or until bubbly. **Yield:** 6 servings.

INDIAN BAKED CORN
Ruby Williams, Bogalusa, Louisiana

Corn is a popular side dish at our family gatherings, and this deliciously different recipe may be why! So colorful and zesty, it's a blue-ribbon winner and a time-tested treasure.

1 package (8-1/2 ounces) corn bread/muffin mix
4 bacon strips, diced
1/3 cup *each* chopped celery, green pepper and onion
1/2 cup plus 2 tablespoons butter, *divided*
1/4 cup milk
1 can (15-1/4 ounces) whole kernel corn, drained
1 can (14-3/4 ounces) cream-style corn
2 tablespoons chopped seeded jalapeno pepper
1 jar (2 ounces) diced pimientos, drained
1 tablespoon sugar
1/2 teaspoon salt

Bake corn bread according to package directions; cool. Crumble enough to measure 2 cups; set aside. In a large skillet, cook bacon over medium heat until crisp. Remove to paper towels; drain, reserving 1 tablespoon drippings. In the drippings, saute celery, green pepper and onion for 2-3 minutes or until tender. Remove from the heat; set aside.

In a saucepan, melt 1/2 cup butter. Stir in the milk, both cans of corn, jalapeno, pimientos, sugar, salt, vegetable mixture and bacon. Add 1 cup corn bread crumbs. Cook for 8-10 minutes or until heated through.

Transfer to a greased 8-in. square baking dish. Melt the remaining butter; toss with the remaining corn bread crumbs. Sprinkle over top. Bake, uncovered, at 350° for 18-20 minutes or until edges are bubbly and top is golden brown. **Yield:** 8 servings.

Editor's Note: When cutting or seeding hot peppers, use gloves to protect your hands. Avoid touching your face.

CARROT CLOVERLEAF ROLLS
Molly Kelly, Gustavus, Alaska

I first tasted these finger-licking, delicately moist rolls at my friend's house—and wouldn't leave without the recipe!

2 cups sliced carrots
1 egg
1/2 cup warm water (110° to 115°), *divided*
1 package (1/4 ounce) active dry yeast
6 tablespoons vegetable oil
1/4 cup sugar
1-1/2 teaspoons molasses
1 teaspoon salt
3-1/4 to 3-3/4 cups all-purpose flour
1 to 2 tablespoons butter, melted

Place carrots in a small saucepan; cover with water. Bring to a boil. Reduce heat; cover and simmer for 8-10 minutes or until tender. Drain and cool slightly. Place carrots in a blender or food processor; cover and process until pureed. Add egg and 1/4 cup warm water; process until blended.

In a large mixing bowl, dissolve yeast in remaining water. Add carrot mixture, oil, sugar, molasses, salt and 2-1/2 cups flour; mix well. Stir in enough remaining flour to form a soft dough. Turn onto a floured surface; knead until smooth and elastic, about 6-8 minutes. Place in a greased bowl, turning once to grease top. Cover and let rise in a warm place until doubled, about 1 hour.

Punch dough down. Turn onto a lightly floured surface; divide into 45 pieces. Shape each into a ball; place three balls in each greased muffin cup. Cover and let rise until doubled, about 30 minutes. Bake at 350° for 18-20 minutes or until lightly browned. Brush with butter. Remove from pans to wire racks. **Yield:** 15 rolls.

WINTER SALAD WITH ORANGE CREAM
Jeanne Spina, Dunedin, Florida
(Pictured above)

This easy-to-make salad has great eye-appeal, and the dressing can be made a day ahead for convenience. It's especially festive-looking with red grapefruit and red pears.

1/2 cup sugar
1 tablespoon cornstarch
1/4 teaspoon salt
1 cup orange juice
1 teaspoon grated orange peel
2 eggs, lightly beaten
1 carton (8 ounces) plain yogurt
1 small bunch romaine
2 medium grapefruit, peeled and sectioned
2 medium navel oranges, peeled and sectioned
2 medium pears, cut into thin wedges
2 medium ripe avocados, peeled and thinly sliced
1 tablespoon lemon juice
1/3 cup chopped walnuts, toasted

In a small saucepan, combine the sugar, cornstarch and salt. Stir in orange juice and peel until blended. Cook and stir over medium-high heat until thickened and bubbly. Reduce heat; cook and stir 2 minutes longer.

Remove from the heat. Stir a small amount of hot mixture into eggs. Return all to the pan, stirring constantly. Bring to a gentle boil; cook and stir 2 minutes longer. Remove from the heat. Cover surface with plastic wrap; cool for 30 minutes without stirring. Fold in yogurt. Cover and refrigerate for at least 2 hours.

Place orange cream in a serving bowl. Place in the center of a 13-in. serving platter. Line platter with romaine leaves; tear remaining romaine and place over leaves. Top with grapefruit and orange sections. Sprinkle pears and avocado with lemon juice; arrange over fruit. Garnish with walnuts. **Yield:** 8-10 servings.

Delectable Desserts

Finish off your Yuletide feast with a flourish of fun fabulous desserts! Guests will carol your praises and be sure to find room for these spectacular once-a-year treats.

SOUR CREAM PLUM PIE
Pat Stueckeman, Garfield, Kansas
(Pictured at left)

Here's a light custardy pie that's one of my "oldies but goodies." It couldn't be much simpler to whip up and makes a refreshing and special finale to any holiday meal.

Pastry for single-crust pie (9 inches)
    2 cans (15 ounces *each*) pitted plums, drained
    2 egg yolks, beaten
    2 cups (16 ounces) sour cream
  1/2 cup sugar
    1 teaspoon vanilla extract

Line a 9-in. pie plate with pastry; flute edges. Line pastry shell with a double thickness of heavy-duty foil. Bake at 450° for 5 minutes. Remove foil; bake 5 minutes longer. Cool on a wire rack. Reduce heat to 350°.

Halve and pit the plums; pat dry with paper towels. Arrange cut side up in crust. In a large bowl, combine egg yolks, sour cream, sugar and vanilla; pour over plums. Cover edges of pastry loosely with foil. Bake for 40-45 minutes or until set. Cool on a wire rack. **Yield:** 6-8 servings.

PEPPERMINT ICE CREAM
Donna Poyner, Canon City, Colorado
(Pictured at left)

Almost too pretty to eat, this refreshing peppermint-pink ice cream is my husband's all-time favorite. It rivals any commercial brand we've tasted and melts all resistance to dessert!

1-1/2 cups sugar
    3 tablespoons all-purpose flour
  1/2 teaspoon salt
    4 cups milk
    4 eggs, beaten
    4 cups heavy whipping cream, *divided*
    2 teaspoons vanilla extract
1-1/2 cups crushed peppermint candies
    3 drops red food coloring

In a large heavy saucepan, combine the sugar, flour and salt. Gradually add milk; stir until smooth. Bring to a boil over medium heat; cook and stir for 2 minutes or until thickened. Remove from the heat; cool slightly.

Whisk a small amount of hot mixture into eggs; return all to the pan, whisking constantly. Cook and stir over low heat until mixture reaches at least 160° and coats the back of a metal spoon.

Remove from the heat. Cool quickly by placing pan in a bowl of ice water; stir for 2 minutes. Press plastic wrap onto surface of custard. Chill for several hours or overnight.

In a blender, combine 1 cup cream, vanilla and crushed

❄ ❄ ❄

DAZZLE 'EM WITH DESSERTS that set a merry mood! Pictured (clockwise from top, p. 32) are a razzle-dazzle Raspberry Ribbon Cake, Sour Cream Plum Pie and luscious Peppermint Ice Cream.

candies; cover and process until candies are finely chopped. In a large bowl, combine the custard, peppermint mixture, food coloring and remaining cream.

Fill ice cream freezer cylinder two-thirds full; freeze according to manufacturer's instructions. Refrigerate remaining mixture until ready to freeze. Remove from the freezer 10 minutes before serving. **Yield:** 2-1/2 quarts.

RASPBERRY RIBBON CAKE
Ruth Lee, Troy, Ontario
(Pictured at left)

I guarantee your guests will exclaim over this showstopper cake. It takes a little extra fussing but never fails to take my family's breath away...every single time!

   12 ounces white baking chocolate, finely chopped
    4 cups heavy whipping cream, *divided*
    4 cups frozen unsweetened raspberries, thawed
BATTER FOR TWO CAKES:
   12 egg yolks
    6 egg whites
    1 cup all-purpose flour
  1/2 teaspoon salt
1-1/2 cups sugar, *divided*
    2 teaspoons vanilla extract, *divided*
  1/2 teaspoon cream of tartar, *divided*
    5 teaspoons unflavored gelatin
  1/4 cup cold water
Fresh raspberries and mint sprigs

Place chocolate in a bowl. In a small saucepan, heat 2 cups cream over medium heat until bubbles form around sides of pan. Pour over chocolate, whisking until melted; whisk in remaining cream. Cover and refrigerate until chilled. Using a fine sieve, press raspberries into a large bowl; discard seeds. Cover and refrigerate until chilled.

For cakes, let egg yolks and whites stand at room temperature for 30 minutes. Sift flour and salt; set aside. For each cake, in a large mixing bowl, beat 6 egg yolks until slightly thickened. Gradually add 1/2 cup sugar, beating until thick and lemon-colored. Beat in 1 teaspoon vanilla. Add 1/2 cup of the flour mixture; mix well.

In another mixing bowl, beat 3 egg whites and 1/4 teaspoon cream of tartar on medium speed until soft peaks form. Gradually beat in 1/4 cup sugar, about 1 tablespoon at a time, on high until stiff glossy peaks form and sugar is dissolved. Fold a fourth of egg whites into the batter, then fold in remaining whites. Gently spoon into a parchment paper-lined 15-in. x 10-in. x 1-in. baking pan; spread evenly. Bake at 350° for 12-15 minutes or until cake springs back when lightly touched. Cool on a wire rack. Repeat for second cake.

For white chocolate whipped cream, in a large mixing bowl, beat 3 cups chilled white chocolate mixture until stiff peaks form; refrigerate. Chill the remaining white chocolate mixture in another large mixing bowl.

For raspberry filling, in a small saucepan, sprinkle gelatin over cold water; let stand for 5 minutes. Dissolve gelatin over medium-low heat, stirring frequently. Stir into strained raspberries.

Place bowl into a large bowl filled with ice water; cool until mixture is syrupy, stirring occasionally. Remove from water bath. Stir 3/4 cup of the reserved white chocolate whipped cream into raspberry mixture; fold in remaining white chocolate whipped cream. Cover and refrigerate for 30 minutes or until set.

To assemble, invert cooled cakes onto wire racks. Trim edges; cut each lengthwise into thirds. Spread one strip with a heaping cup of raspberry filling to within 1 in. of short sides and 1/2 in. of long sides. Starting at a short end, roll up. Stand on end in center of serving plate. Spread remaining raspberry mixture over remaining strips. Working with one strip at a time, and starting at the edge of the last strip, coil around center roll. Cover and refrigerate.

For frosting, beat reserved white chocolate mixture until stiff peaks form. Spread over top and sides of cake. Refrigerate for 1-2 hours. Garnish with raspberries and mint. **Yield:** 12-16 servings.

CHOCOLATE-CHEESECAKE CREAM PUFFS
Lisa Cooper, Caistor Centre, Ontario

I always get compliments from the chocolate lovers at my table when I serve these dainty puffs.

    1 cup water
  1/2 cup butter
    1 cup all-purpose flour
    4 eggs
FILLING:
    1 cup (6 ounces) semisweet chocolate chips
    1 package (8 ounces) cream cheese, softened
  1/2 cup confectioners' sugar
    2 cups heavy whipping cream
GLAZE:
  1/3 cup semisweet chocolate chips
    1 tablespoon shortening

In a large saucepan, bring water and butter to a boil. Add flour all at once, stirring until a smooth ball forms. Remove from the heat; let stand for 5 minutes. Add eggs, one at a time, beating well after each addition. Continue beating until mixture is smooth and shiny.

Drop 12 rounded tablespoonfuls 3 in. apart onto a greased baking sheet. Bake at 400° for 30-35 minutes or until golden brown. Transfer to a wire rack. Immediately cut a slit in each puff to allow steam to escape; cool. Split puffs and set tops aside; remove soft dough from inside. Cool.

For filling, melt chocolate chips in a microwave; set aside. In a mixing bowl, beat cream cheese and confectioners' sugar until smooth. Beat in melted chocolate. In another bowl, beat cream until stiff peaks form; gradually beat into chocolate mixture. Spoon into cream puffs; replace tops. For glaze, melt chocolate chips and shortening in a microwave. Drizzle over puffs. **Yield:** 1 dozen.

Dessert Tip

• Try grating a chocolate candy bar or candy canes over the top of whipped cream on your chocolate desserts. It's as pretty and festive as it is delicious.

LINZER TART
Karen Ehatt, Chester, Maryland
(Pictured above)

This lovely versatile tart shows up regularly at family gatherings. I can customize it for any holiday occasion by using different-shaped cookie cutouts...or different fruit fillings. And even my picky children gobble it up!

  1/2 cup butter, softened
  3/4 cup sugar
  1/2 teaspoon grated lemon peel
    1 egg
  1/2 cup slivered almonds, toasted
1-1/2 cups all-purpose flour
    1 teaspoon ground cinnamon
  1/4 teaspoon salt
    1 jar (18 ounces) raspberry preserves

In a mixing bowl, cream the butter, sugar and lemon peel for 5 minutes. Add egg; mix well. Place almonds in a blender or food processor; cover and process until ground. Combine the ground almonds, flour, cinnamon and salt; gradually beat into creamed mixture. Remove 1/3 cup of dough. Roll between two sheets of waxed paper to 1/8-in. thickness. Freeze for 8-10 minutes or until firm.

Press remaining dough evenly onto the bottom and up the sides of an ungreased 11-in. fluted tart pan with removable bottom. Spread raspberry preserves over crust. Remove remaining dough from freezer; using small cookie cutters, cut out desired shapes. Place over preserves.

Bake at 375° for 20-25 minutes or until crust is golden brown and filling is bubbly. Cool for 10 minutes. Loosen sides of pan. Cool completely on a wire rack. Remove sides of pan. **Yield:** 10-12 servings.

WALNUT MINCEMEAT PIE
Mary Reagan, Warsaw, New York

Here's a tasty twist on the more traditional mincemeat pie. This one's sweeter, creamier, easier to make and so yummy!

Pastry for single-crust pie (9 inches)
    1 cup sugar
    2 tablespoons all-purpose flour
  1/8 teaspoon salt
    3 eggs, beaten
  1/4 cup butter, melted
    1 cup prepared mincemeat
  1/2 cup chopped walnuts

Line a 9-in. pie plate with pastry; flute edges. Line pastry shell with a double thickness of heavy-duty foil. Bake at 450° for 5 minutes. Remove foil; bake 5 minutes longer. Cool on a wire rack. Reduce heat to 350°.

In a bowl, combine the sugar, flour and salt. Stir in the eggs, butter, mincemeat and walnuts until blended. Pour into crust. Bake for 40-45 minutes or until a knife inserted near the center comes out clean (cover edges loosely with foil if necessary to prevent overbrowning). Cool on a wire rack. **Yield:** 6-8 servings.

CHOCOLATE BREAD PUDDING
Laurie Haight, New Hope, Minnesota

This is one dessert made with busy Yuletide hostesses in mind. It's festive, rich, a cinch to prepare and feeds a crowd!

3-3/4 cups milk
    3 squares (1 ounce *each*) unsweetened chocolate
  1/2 teaspoon salt
    2 eggs
    2 egg yolks
  3/4 cup sugar
    1 teaspoon vanilla extract
  1/4 teaspoon almond extract
    5 slices day-old bread, cut into 1-inch cubes
MERINGUE:
    2 egg whites
  1/4 cup sugar

In a large saucepan, heat the milk, chocolate and salt over low heat, stirring until chocolate is melted. Whisk until smooth; cool slightly. In a large mixing bowl, beat the eggs, yolks and sugar until smooth; add extracts. Gradually beat in chocolate mixture. Place the bread cubes in a bowl; add the chocolate mixture. Let stand for 10 minutes, stirring occasionally.

Transfer to a greased 11-in. x 7-in. x 2-in. baking dish. Place dish in a 13-in. x 9-in. x 2-in. baking pan. Fill larger pan with boiling water to a depth of 1 in. Bake, uncovered, at 400° for 40 minutes.

For meringue, in a mixing bowl, beat egg whites on medium speed until foamy. Beat in sugar, 1 tablespoon at a time, on high until soft peaks form and sugar is dissolved.

Remove the bread pudding from the oven. Reduce heat to 350°. Spoon meringue around edges of pudding. Bake 15 minutes longer or until meringue is lightly browned. Serve warm. Refrigerate leftovers. **Yield:** 8-10 servings.

TRIPLE-LAYER ICE BOMBE
Petra Maria, Oakland, California
(Pictured below)

Whether you like your holiday desserts fa-la-la festive or ooh-la-la fancy, this one's for you! The creamy frozen concoction is so stunning, it's reserved strictly for Christmas and birthdays at our house. Sometimes we substitute raspberry sorbet and dark chocolate ice cream.

    2 pints strawberry ice cream, softened
    2 pints chocolate ice cream, softened
    2 cups heavy whipping cream, *divided*
  1/2 cup sugar
    4 egg yolks
    2 teaspoons vanilla extract
    1 cup chopped hazelnuts, toasted
    1 Toblerone candy bar (3.52 ounces), chopped
  1/2 cup dried currants
1-2/3 cups semisweet chocolate chips
    1 tablespoon shortening

Line a 4-qt. bowl with plastic wrap. Place in the freezer for 30 minutes. Quickly spread strawberry ice cream over the bottom and up the sides to within 1/2 in. of the top of bowl. Freeze for 1 hour or until firm. Repeat with chocolate ice cream. Freeze for 2 hours or until firm.

Meanwhile, in a small heavy saucepan, combine 1/2 cup whipping cream, sugar and egg yolks. Cook and stir over medium heat until mixture reaches at least 160° and coats the back of a metal spoon. Remove from the heat; stir in vanilla. Refrigerate until chilled.

Fold in the hazelnuts, chopped candy bar and currants. Beat remaining whipping cream until stiff peaks form; fold into custard. Spoon into ice cream shell, spreading to completely cover the top. Cover and freeze overnight.

In a microwave, melt chocolate chips and shortening; stir until smooth. Cool. Remove bombe from the freezer and invert onto a serving plate. Remove bowl and plastic wrap. Working quickly, spread chocolate, a little at a time, over entire bombe. Freeze until chocolate is firm. Cut into wedges. **Yield:** 12-14 servings.

Show your good taste with homemade gifts for friends and busy hostesses…
from snack fixin's and cookie mixin's to yummy breads and spreads.

WILD RICE AND BARLEY SOUP MIX
Country Woman Test Kitchen
(Pictured at left)

Warm up your loved ones on frosty winter nights with this hearty, stick-to-the-ribs soup mix. Layered in pretty bow-tied jars, it looks as good as it tastes. Include prep instructions!

> 1 tablespoon brown sugar
> 2 teaspoons Italian seasoning
> 1/2 teaspoon dried minced garlic
> 1/2 teaspoon ground celery seed
> 1/2 teaspoon pepper
> 1/2 cup medium pearl barley
> 1/3 cup dried vegetable flakes
> 3 tablespoons chicken bouillon granules
> 1/2 cup uncooked wild rice
> 1/2 cup dried minced onion
> **ADDITIONAL INGREDIENTS:**
> 8 cups water
> Real bacon bits, optional

In a small bowl, combine the first five ingredients. In a pint-size jar with a tight-fitting lid, layer the barley, vegetable flakes, brown sugar mixture, bouillon, rice and onion, packing each layer tightly (do not mix). Cover and store in a cool dry place for up to 4 months.

To prepare soup: Pour mix into a large saucepan. Add 8 cups of water and bring to a boil. Reduce heat; cover and simmer for 1 hour or until rice is tender. Garnish with bacon bits if desired. **Yield:** 6 servings.

CHOCOLATY CHRISTMAS SNACK MIX
Janet Hall, Maple Heights, Ohio
(Pictured at left)

I love giving Yuletide gifts from my kitchen to everyone I know. This recipe is one folks ask for year after year. You can vary the fruits and nuts—and it seems to suit all ages.

> 1 pound dry roasted peanuts
> 1 pound mixed nuts
> 3 cups red and green crispy M&M's
> 2 cups red and green milk chocolate M&M's
> 1 package (12 ounces) semisweet chocolate chips
> 1 package (11-1/2 ounces) milk chocolate chips
> 1 package (10 to 11 ounces) butterscotch chips
> 1 package (10 to 12 ounces) vanilla *or* white chips
> 1 package (10 ounces) peanut butter chips
> 1-1/2 cups chocolate-covered raisins
> 1-1/2 cups raisins

In a large bowl, combine all ingredients. Store in airtight containers or plastic bags. **Yield:** 22 cups.

❄ ❄ ❄

GIFTS MONEY CAN'T BUY. Who on your list wouldn't savor a homemade, heartfelt gift of (clockwise from top left, p. 36) Chocolaty Christmas Snack Mix, Wild Rice and Barley Soup Mix, or Cranberry Scones?

CRANBERRY SCONES
Linda Burnett, Stanton, California
(Pictured at left)

Being an Anglophile, I've tried lots of scone recipes over the years, but this is my all-time favorite. It was given to me by a hotel chef in Los Angeles and bakes into batches of lovely Christmas gifts for friends and family.

> 2 cups all-purpose flour
> 2 tablespoons sugar
> 2 teaspoons baking powder
> 1/4 teaspoon salt
> 1/2 cup shortening
> 1 egg, beaten
> 2/3 cup heavy whipping cream
> 1/3 cup dried cranberries *or* currants

In a large bowl, combine the flour, sugar, baking powder and salt. Cut in shortening until mixture resembles coarse crumbs. Combine egg and cream; stir into crumb mixture just until blended. Stir in cranberries. Turn onto a floured surface; knead gently four times.

Shape dough into a ball; place on an ungreased baking sheet. Pat into an 8-in. circle. With a sharp knife, score the dough into eight wedges (do not separate). Bake at 425° for 15-20 minutes or until golden brown. Break into wedges. Serve warm. **Yield:** 8 scones.

RAISIN GINGERBREAD MUFFINS
Laureen Whitacre, South Bend, Indiana

These muffins are my husband's favorite year-round. He likes them warm and topped with cream cheese and confectioners' sugar. I like them because they're easy to make and they freeze beautifully.

> 1/2 cup butter, softened
> 1/2 cup sugar
> 2 eggs
> 1/2 cup sour cream
> 1/2 cup molasses
> 2 cups plus 1 tablespoon all-purpose flour, *divided*
> 1 teaspoon baking soda
> 1 teaspoon ground ginger
> 1/4 teaspoon ground allspice
> 1/4 teaspoon ground cinnamon
> 1/2 cup golden raisins

In a large mixing bowl, cream butter and sugar. Add eggs, one at a time, beating well after each addition. Beat in sour cream and molasses. Combine 2 cups flour, baking soda, ginger, allspice and cinnamon; add to creamed mixture just until moistened. Toss the raisins with the remaining flour; stir into batter.

Fill paper-lined muffin cups three-fourths full. Bake at 375° for 18-20 minutes or until a toothpick comes out clean. Cool for 5 minutes before removing from pans to wire racks. **Yield:** about 1 dozen.

VICTORIAN PLUM CONSERVE
Pearl White, Ancaster, Ontario

This old-fashioned spicy treat is wonderful spread on scones and toast, used as a tart filling, or served with poultry and ham.

  3 medium navel oranges
 12 ripe plums (about 4 pounds), pitted and
    coarsely chopped
1-1/2 cups raisins
  1 cup chopped peeled ripe pears
  3 cups sugar
  1/4 teaspoon ground allspice
  1/4 teaspoon ground cinnamon

Grate the peel from the oranges, reserving the peel (about 1/3 cup). Peel off and discard white membrane; section the oranges. In a large saucepan or Dutch oven, combine the orange sections and peel, plums, raisins, pears, sugar, allspice and cinnamon. Bring to a boil. Reduce heat; cook for 1 hour or until thickened, stirring frequently.

Pour hot mixture into hot sterilized jars, leaving 1/4-in. headspace. Adjust caps. Process for 15 minutes in a boiling-water bath. **Yield:** 9 half-pints.

PEANUT BUTTER POPCORN
Mary Shrivers, Ada, Oklahoma
(Pictured above)

A friend shared this fast-to-fix recipe with me and I've been making gift batches ever since. It's a perfect family snack when snuggling up to watch classic Christmas movies together!

3-1/2 quarts popped popcorn
  1 cup sugar
  1 cup honey
  1 cup peanut butter

Place the popcorn in a large bowl and set aside. In a heavy saucepan, bring sugar and honey to a boil over medium heat, stirring constantly. Boil and stir for 5 minutes. Remove from the heat; stir in peanut butter until blended.

Pour over popcorn and toss gently to coat. Turn onto waxed paper; cool completely. Store in airtight containers or plastic bags. **Yield:** 14 servings.

GRANDMA'S CHUNKY PEANUT BUTTER
Noble Winstead, Tuscaloosa, Alabama

I think this creamy peanut butter with just a hint of orange flavor is truly Yuletide-special. I tie small jars with colorful ribbons to make great stocking stuffers or last-minute gifts.

1-3/4 cups peanuts
  1/4 teaspoon salt, optional
  1/4 teaspoon grated orange peel, optional

Chop 1/4 cup peanuts and set aside. Place the remaining peanuts in a blender or food processor. Cover and process for 5 minutes or until smooth and spreadable, occasionally scraping sides of bowl. Stir in the chopped peanuts. Add salt and orange peel if desired. Cover and refrigerate for 1 hour. May be refrigerated for up to 1 month. **Yield:** 1 cup.

MOCHA COFFEE MIX
Virginia Krites, Cridersville, Ohio

Whether I use regular or decaf crystals, everyone I know gives this creamy coffee-and-chocolate blend rave reviews. It's easy to mix, put in pretty jars and keep on hand for hostess gifts.

  1 cup powdered nondairy creamer
3/4 cup sugar
  1/2 cup instant coffee granules
  2 tablespoons baking cocoa
ADDITIONAL INGREDIENTS (for each batch):
  1 cup boiling water

In a blender or food processor, combine the creamer, sugar, coffee granules and cocoa. Cover and process until fine. Transfer to an airtight container. Store in a cool dry place for up to 1 year. **Yield:** 8 servings (2 cups total).

To prepare mocha coffee: Place 1/4 cup mix in a mug; add boiling water and stir until dissolved.

WHITE CHIP-CRANBERRY GRANOLA BARS
Janis Loomis, Madison, Virginia

Tasty and nutritious, these chewy high-energy snack bars are great for road trips, lunch boxes, late-night snacks or to get college kids through exams and into the Christmas spirit!

  1/4 cup maple syrup
  1/4 cup honey
  1/4 cup packed brown sugar
  2 tablespoons peanut butter
  1 egg white
  1 tablespoon evaporated milk
  1 teaspoon vanilla extract
  1 cup whole wheat flour
1/2 teaspoon baking soda

1/2 teaspoon ground cinnamon
2 cups old-fashioned oats
1-1/2 cups crisp rice cereal
1/2 cup vanilla *or* white chips
1/2 cup dried cranberries
1/4 cup chopped walnuts

In a large mixing bowl, combine the syrup, honey, brown sugar, peanut butter, egg white, milk and vanilla; beat until smooth. Combine the flour, baking soda and cinnamon; stir into syrup mixture. Fold in the oats, cereal, chips, cranberries and walnuts.

Press into a greased 13-in. x 9-in. x 2-in. baking pan. Bake at 350° for 18-20 minutes or until golden brown. Cool on a wire rack. Cut into bars. Store in an airtight container. **Yield:** 2 dozen.

CHRISTMAS BATTER BREAD
Dawn Winkler, Montrose, Colorado

With or without the frosting, slices of this fruit-filled bread add a holiday flair to ordinary breakfasts. I like to wrap gift loaves in cellophane topped with curly ribbons.

2 packages (1/4 ounce *each*) active dry yeast
2-1/2 cups warm water (110° to 115°)
1/4 cup butter, softened
1/4 cup sugar
2 teaspoons salt
1 teaspoon ground cinnamon
1/2 teaspoon ground nutmeg
1/4 teaspoon ground cloves
5-3/4 to 6-1/4 cups all-purpose flour
1/2 cup chopped candied fruit
1/2 cup raisins
1/2 cup chopped walnuts *or* pecans
GLAZE:
1 cup confectioners' sugar
1 to 2 tablespoons milk

In a large mixing bowl, dissolve yeast in warm water. Add the butter, sugar, salt, cinnamon, nutmeg, cloves and 3 cups flour. Beat on medium speed for 2 minutes. Add enough remaining flour to form a firm batter. Stir in candied fruit, raisins and nuts. Do not knead. Cover and let rise in a warm place until doubled, about 30 minutes.

Stir dough down. Transfer to two greased 9-in. x 5-in. x 3-in. loaf pans. Cover and let rise until doubled, about 40 minutes. Bake at 375° for 40-45 minutes or until golden brown. Remove from pans to wire racks to cool. Combine glaze ingredients; drizzle over bread. **Yield:** 2 loaves.

Wrapping It Up

Looking for a dazzling presentation for homemade treats this holiday season? Use tinted cellophane, seasonal fabrics in Christmas colors or nylon netting for unique gift wraps. Then spruce up your jars, baskets and boxes with bright yarns, raffia or inexpensive chenille stems and snips of rickrack.

CHERRY BROWNIE CUPS
Rebecca Brown, Cumberland, Maryland
(Pictured below)

I like to lavish the chocolate lovers on my gift list with small Christmas tins of these cheery, cherry-topped treats.

3/4 cup butter, cubed
2 squares (1 ounce *each*) unsweetened chocolate, chopped
2 cups sugar
4 eggs
1 teaspoon vanilla extract
1 cup all-purpose flour
FUDGE FILLING:
1 package (3 ounces) cream cheese, softened
1 teaspoon vanilla extract
1/4 cup corn syrup
1-1/2 squares (1-1/2 ounces) unsweetened chocolate, melted and cooled
1 cup confectioners' sugar
1 jar (10 ounces) maraschino cherries with stems, drained and patted dry

Place the butter and chocolate in a microwave-safe bowl; cover and microwave on high for 1-2 minutes or until melted. Stir in sugar until dissolved. Transfer to a mixing bowl. Add eggs, one at a time, beating well after each addition. Stir in vanilla and flour.

Fill paper-lined miniature muffin cups two-thirds full. Bake at 350° for 20-22 minutes or until a toothpick comes out clean. Cool for 5 minutes. With the end of a wooden spoon handle, make a 1/2-in. indentation in the top of each brownie; remove from pans to wire racks to cool completely.

For filling, in a large mixing bowl, beat cream cheese and vanilla until smooth. Beat in corn syrup and melted chocolate until well blended. Add confectioners' sugar and beat until smooth. Spoon 1 teaspoon of filling in the center of each brownie. Top with a cherry. Store in the refrigerator. **Yield:** 5 dozen.

Cookie Cavalcade

CHRISTMAS COLLECTION (clockwise from far left): Mocha Cookie Pretzels (p. 42), Chocolate-Dipped Maple Logs (p. 42), Peppermint Twist Kisses (p. 43), No-Bake Spruce Cookies (p. 42) and Brown Sugar Cutouts (p. 42).

Bake a batch of merry memories from Christmases past with old-fashioned bars and homemade Christmas cookies decked out in seasonal splendor!

MOCHA COOKIE PRETZELS
Country Woman Test Kitchen
(Pictured on page 40)

Looking for a little something special to bake up for the holidays? Try these elegant mocha-frosted cookies our Test Kitchen created. They're wonderful with coffee and make an eye-catching addition to any cookie platter.

  1/2 cup butter, softened
  1/2 cup sugar
    1 egg
    2 squares (1 ounce *each*) unsweetened chocolate, melted and cooled
    1 teaspoon vanilla extract
    2 cups cake flour
  1/4 teaspoon salt
GLAZE:
    1 cup (6 ounces) semisweet chocolate chips
    1 teaspoon shortening
    1 teaspoon light corn syrup
    1 cup confectioners' sugar
    3 to 5 tablespoons strong brewed coffee
    2 squares (1 ounce *each*) white baking chocolate, chopped
Green colored sugar, optional

In a small mixing bowl, cream butter and sugar. Beat in egg. Beat in melted chocolate and vanilla. Combine flour and salt; gradually add to creamed mixture. Cover and refrigerate for 1 hour or until easy to handle.

Divide dough into fourths; divide each portion into 12 pieces. Shape each piece into a 6-in. rope; twist into a pretzel shape. Place 1 in. apart on lightly greased baking sheets. Bake at 400° for 7-9 minutes or until set. Remove to wire racks to cool.

For glaze, in a microwave, melt the chocolate chips, shortening and corn syrup; stir until smooth. Stir in confectioners' sugar and enough coffee to achieve desired consistency. Dip cookies in glaze; allow excess to drip off. Place on waxed paper until set.

In a microwave, melt white chocolate; stir until smooth. Drizzle over cookies. Decorate with green sugar if desired; let stand until set. **Yield:** 4 dozen.

NO-BAKE SPRUCE COOKIES
Jeanette Alessi, Orange, California
(Pictured on page 41)

These easy treats won first prize at our last cookie exchange for "prettiest and best tasting" cookie! They're fun to make, and your kids will like trimming them with red-hot candy ornaments.

    36 large marshmallows
  1/2 cup butter, cubed
    1 to 2 teaspoons green food coloring
    1 teaspoon almond extract
    4 cups cornflakes
Red-hot candies
   12 Tootsie Roll Midgees, cut in half, optional

In a heavy saucepan, combine the marshmallows, butter, food coloring and almond extract. Cook and stir over low heat until smooth. Remove from the heat; gently stir in cornflakes until well coated. Drop by tablespoonfuls onto waxed paper.

Using a 3-in. Christmas tree cookie cutter, shape into trees. Add red-hots for ornaments. Press a Tootsie Roll half into the base for tree trunk if desired. **Yield:** about 2 dozen.

BROWN SUGAR CUTOUTS
Norma Mueller, Milwaukee, Wisconsin
(Pictured on page 40)

I bake so many cookies for the holidays that I have one recipe box just for cookies alone! But of all of them, these simple cutouts are among my husband's flavor favorites.

    1 cup butter, softened
    2 cups packed brown sugar
    3 eggs
    2 teaspoons grated lemon peel
    3 cups all-purpose flour
    1 teaspoon baking soda
    1 teaspoon ground ginger
FROSTING:
1-1/2 cups confectioners' sugar
  1/2 teaspoon vanilla extract
    2 to 3 tablespoons half-and-half cream
Green food coloring, optional

In a large mixing bowl, cream butter and brown sugar. Add the eggs and lemon peel; beat well. Combine the flour, baking soda and ginger; gradually add to creamed mixture and mix well. Cover and refrigerate for 2 hours or until easy to handle.

On a floured surface, roll out dough to 1/8-in. thickness. Cut with 2-in. cookie cutters. Place 2 in. apart on ungreased baking sheets. Bake at 350° for 8-10 minutes or until golden brown. Remove to wire racks to cool.

For frosting, in a bowl, combine confectioners' sugar, vanilla and enough cream to achieve spreading consistency. Add food coloring if desired to some or all of the frosting. Decorate cookies. **Yield:** about 6 dozen.

CHOCOLATE-DIPPED MAPLE LOGS
Lorraine Caland, Thunder Bay, Ontario
(Pictured on page 40)

For as long as I can remember, these fancy little maple logs have been a Christmas tradition at our house. My girls loved working the assembly line and dipping the ends in chocolate.

  1/2 cup butter, softened
  1/2 cup shortening
  1/2 cup confectioners' sugar
    1 teaspoon vanilla extract
    1 teaspoon maple flavoring
1-1/2 cups all-purpose flour
    1 cup quick-cooking oats

    1/2 teaspoon salt
      1 cup (6 ounces) semisweet chocolate chips
      3 tablespoons milk
    3/4 cup ground walnuts

In a large mixing bowl, cream the butter, shortening and confectioners' sugar. Beat in vanilla and maple flavoring. Combine the flour, oats and salt; gradually add to creamed mixture.

On a lightly floured surface, shape dough into 1/2-in.-wide logs. Cut into 2-in. pieces. Place 1 in. apart on ungreased baking sheets. Bake at 325° for 15-18 minutes or until set and very lightly browned. Remove to wire racks to cool.

In a microwave, melt chocolate chips and milk; stir until smooth. Dip one end of each cookie into chocolate, then roll in walnuts. Place on waxed paper until set. **Yield:** about 6 dozen.

PEPPERMINT TWIST KISSES
Traci Krick, Bear, Delaware
(Pictured on page 41)

As rosy as Santa's cheeks, these merry morsels with the chocolate kiss on top are a delightful Yuletide favorite and one of my most-requested recipes.

    1/2 cup butter, softened
    1/3 cup sugar
      1 egg yolk
    1/2 teaspoon peppermint extract
    1/2 teaspoon vanilla extract
  1-1/4 cups all-purpose flour
    1/4 teaspoon salt
      4 to 8 drops red food coloring
     36 chocolate kisses

In a large mixing bowl, cream butter and sugar. Add the egg yolk and extracts; mix well. Combine flour and salt; gradually add to creamed mixture. Divide dough in half; tint one portion red. Divide each into four portions. Cover and refrigerate for 1 hour.

Shape each portion into a 9-in. log. Place one red log next to one white log; twist gently to create one swirled roll. Roll gently until roll becomes one log. Repeat with remaining dough.

Cut each log into nine slices; roll each into a ball. Place 1 in. apart on ungreased baking sheets. Flatten slightly with a glass. Bake at 350° for 10-12 minutes until edges are lightly browned. Press chocolate kisses into the center of warm cookies. Remove to wire racks to cool. **Yield:** 3 dozen.

Cookie Tips

• Use your electric knife to easily cut rolled and chilled cookie dough. You will get perfectly even cookies every time.

• Save the paper wrapping from sticks of butter and store in the freezer. When a recipe calls for a greased pan or cookie sheet, rub with one of the wrappings.

• Freeze unbaked cookie dough for up to 4 months.

RASPBERRY TREASURES
Country Woman Test Kitchen
(Pictured above)

Light and flaky, these delicate fruit-filled cookies have the look of petite and elegant pastries. We like them with a spot of raspberry or apricot filling—and a cup of Christmas tea.

    1/2 cup butter, softened
      1 package (3 ounces) cream cheese, softened
      1 teaspoon vanilla extract
      1 cup all-purpose flour
    1/8 teaspoon salt
    1/2 cup raspberry filling
      1 egg
      1 teaspoon water

In a large mixing bowl, cream butter and cream cheese. Beat in vanilla. Combine flour and salt; add to creamed mixture. Divide dough in half; wrap each portion in plastic wrap. Refrigerate for 1 hour or until easy to handle.

On a lightly floured surface, roll out dough to 1/8-in. thickness. Cut with a floured 3-in. round cookie cutter. Place 1 teaspoon raspberry filling in the center of each. Bring three edges together over filling, overlapping slightly (a small amount of filling will show); pinch edges gently. In a small bowl, beat egg and water; brush over dough.

Place 1 in. apart on ungreased baking sheets. Bake at 375° for 10-12 minutes or until golden brown. Cool for 1 minute before removing to wire racks. **Yield:** 2 dozen.

Editor's Note: This recipe was tested with Solo filling.

TOFFEE ALMOND COOKIES
Connie Vincent, Sargent, Nebraska
(Pictured above)

These lovely little layered treats boast a buttery bottom and soft toffee top with a sprinkling of almonds. One recipe even makes enough to set some aside for company...if Santa doesn't get to them first!

    3/4 cup butter, softened
    1/2 cup packed brown sugar
      1 egg yolk
      1 teaspoon vanilla extract
    1/2 teaspoon salt, *divided*
  1-1/2 cups all-purpose flour
  1-1/2 cups butterscotch chips
    1/4 cup light corn syrup
      2 tablespoons shortening
      1 tablespoon water
    1/2 cup slivered almonds, toasted

In a large mixing bowl, cream butter and brown sugar. Beat in the egg yolk, vanilla and 1/4 teaspoon salt; stir in flour. Spread evenly into a greased 13-in. x 9-in. x 2-in. baking pan. Bake at 350° for 18-20 minutes or until lightly browned. Cool slightly.

Meanwhile, in a microwave-safe bowl, combine the butterscotch chips, corn syrup, shortening, water and remaining salt. Cover and microwave at 50% power until chocolate is melted, stirring every 30 seconds. Spread over crust. Sprinkle with almonds. Refrigerate until set before cutting. **Yield:** about 4 dozen.

CHERRY WALNUT BARS
Margaret Zuber, Marietta, Georgia

Post some holiday cheer with these nutty little fruit bars that travel extremely well. Since our cookie-loving son joined the Air Force, I've shipped them as far away as England and Italy.

  2-1/4 cups all-purpose flour
    1/2 cup sugar
      1 cup cold butter, cubed
      2 eggs
      1 cup packed brown sugar
    1/2 teaspoon salt
    1/2 teaspoon baking powder
    1/2 teaspoon vanilla extract
      1 jar (6 ounces) maraschino cherries
    1/2 cup chopped walnuts
ICING:
      1 cup confectioners' sugar
      1 tablespoon butter, softened
    1/2 cup flaked coconut, toasted, optional

In a large bowl, combine flour and sugar. Cut in butter until mixture resembles coarse crumbs. Pat into an ungreased 13-in. x 9-in. x 2-in. baking pan. Bake at 350° for 18-22 minutes or until edges are lightly browned.

Meanwhile, in a small bowl, combine the eggs, brown sugar, salt, baking powder and vanilla. Drain cherries, reserving 2 tablespoons juice; set juice aside. Chop cherries; add to brown sugar mixture. Stir in walnuts. Pour over crust and spread evenly. Bake 20-25 minutes longer or until set. Cool completely on a wire rack.

For icing, combine confectioners' sugar and butter in a mixing bowl. Add enough reserved cherry juice to achieve desired consistency; drizzle over bars. Sprinkle with coconut if desired. **Yield:** 4 dozen.

PUMPKIN DROP COOKIES
Priscilla Anderson, Salt Lake City, Utah

Packed with the flavors of Christmases past, these pumpkin drop cookies with caramel frosting are simply scrumptious and as much a part of our holidays as mistletoe and carols! They are a great way to use our home-canned pumpkin.

      1 cup butter, softened
    1/2 cup sugar
    1/2 cup packed brown sugar
      1 egg
      1 cup canned pumpkin
      2 teaspoons vanilla extract
      2 cups all-purpose flour
      1 teaspoon baking powder
      1 teaspoon baking soda
      1 teaspoon ground cinnamon
    1/2 teaspoon salt
    3/4 cup chopped pecans
PENUCHE FROSTING:
      3 tablespoons brown sugar
      2 tablespoons butter
      3 tablespoons milk
  1-3/4 to 2 cups confectioners' sugar

In a large mixing bowl, cream butter and sugars. Beat in egg. Add pumpkin and vanilla. Combine the flour, baking powder, baking soda, cinnamon and salt; gradually add to creamed mixture. Stir in pecans.

Drop by rounded teaspoonfuls 2 in. apart onto ungreased baking sheets. Bake at 350° for 11-13 minutes or until edges are lightly browned. Remove to wire racks to cool.

For frosting, in a small saucepan, bring brown sugar and butter to a boil. Cook and stir over medium heat for 1 minute. Remove from the heat; cool for 10 minutes. Transfer to a large mixing bowl; beat in milk. Beat in enough confectioners' sugar to achieve spreading consistency. Frost cookies. **Yield:** about 5 dozen.

STRAWBERRY CHEESECAKE BARS
Melinda McConnell, Flint, Michigan

Although these bars are Christmas-party pretty, they're really good any time of year. In fact, I always double the recipe because they're such a hit with my husband and six children. Even then, I never have any left over.

- 1 tube (18 ounces) refrigerated sugar cookie dough
- 1 package (8 ounces) cream cheese, softened
- 1 cup (8 ounces) sour cream
- 1/4 cup sugar
- 1 egg, beaten
- 1/2 teaspoon vanilla extract
- 1 jar (12 ounces) strawberry preserves

Cut cookie dough into 25 slices. Arrange side by side in an ungreased 13-in. x 9-in. x 2-in. baking pan. Pat together to close gaps. Bake at 375° for 18-20 minutes or until lightly browned and edges are firm to the touch.

Meanwhile, in a large mixing bowl, beat the cream cheese, sour cream and sugar. Add egg and vanilla; mix well. Spread preserves over warm crust. Carefully spread cream cheese mixture evenly over preserves.

Bake for 25-30 minutes or until a toothpick inserted near the center comes out clean. Cool on a wire rack. Cut into bars. Refrigerate leftovers. **Yield:** 2 dozen.

CRANBERRY MACAROONS
Jane Guilbeau, Melbourne, Florida

A doily-lined tray piled high with these cookies never fails to draw exclamations of admiration from all who see them. Crunchy on the outside and chewy on the inside, the cookies have a wonderful taste and texture.

- 4 egg whites
- 1/4 teaspoon cream of tartar
- 1 teaspoon almond extract
- 1-1/3 cups sugar
- 2 drops red food coloring, optional
- 1 cup sliced almonds, chopped
- 3/4 cup flaked coconut
- 1/2 cup finely chopped dried cranberries
- 3 cups cornflakes, finely crushed

In a large mixing bowl, beat the egg whites, cream of tartar and almond extract on medium speed until soft peaks form. Gradually beat in sugar, 2 tablespoons at a time, on high until stiff glossy peaks form. Add food coloring if desired. Fold in the almonds, coconut, cranberries and cornflakes.

Drop by rounded teaspoonfuls 2 in. apart onto well-greased baking sheets. Bake at 325° for 20-22 minutes. Remove to wire racks to cool. **Yield:** about 4-1/2 dozen.

OATMEAL SHORTBREAD
Lillian Machacek, Taber, Alberta

Crunchy oats give this traditional shortbread recipe a new twist. These buttery confections are simply good to the very last crumb—especially with a cup of hot coffee or eggnog. I've also learned that they keep for months...if you hide them well enough!

- 1-1/2 cups butter, softened
- 3/4 cup sugar
- 1 cup quick-cooking oats
- 2-3/4 cups all-purpose flour
- 1/2 teaspoon ground cinnamon
- 1/4 teaspoon salt
- Additional sugar

In a large mixing bowl, cream butter and sugar. Place the oats in a blender or food processor; process until ground. Add to creamed mixture.

Combine the flour, cinnamon and salt; gradually add to oat mixture. Cover and refrigerate for 1 hour.

Roll dough into 1-in. balls; roll in sugar. Place 2 in. apart on ungreased baking sheets; flatten slightly. Bake at 325° for 15-20 minutes or until golden brown. Remove to wire racks to cool. **Yield:** about 4-1/2 dozen.

FROSTED CASHEW DROPS
Lois McGrady, Hillsville, Virginia

If your family likes the taste of cashews, they will love these caramel-flavored cookies. I think they make a nice nutty addition to any holiday cookie platter, but they always disappear quickly no matter what time of year I decide to serve them.

- 1/2 cup butter, softened
- 1 cup packed brown sugar
- 1/2 cup sour cream
- 1 egg
- 1 teaspoon vanilla extract
- 1-3/4 cups all-purpose flour
- 1 teaspoon baking powder
- 1/2 teaspoon baking soda
- 1/4 teaspoon salt
- 1 cup salted cashews, chopped and toasted
- **FROSTING:**
- 1/4 cup butter, cubed
- 2 cups confectioners' sugar
- 2 to 3 tablespoons milk

In a large mixing bowl, cream the butter and brown sugar; beat in the sour cream, egg and vanilla. Combine the flour, baking powder, baking soda and salt; gradually add to creamed mixture. Stir in the cashews.

Drop by rounded tablespoonfuls onto greased baking sheets. Bake at 375° for 8-10 minutes or until lightly browned. Remove to wire racks to cool.

For frosting, in a heavy saucepan, cook the butter over medium heat for 7-9 minutes or until golden brown. Whisk in the confectioners' sugar and enough milk to achieve a smooth consistency. Spread over cooled cookies. **Yield:** about 4 dozen.

Sugarplum Sweets

Treat family and friends to high-stepping holiday style with a bounty of bonbons, Christmas confections and trays of incredible edibles!

MOCHA TRUFFLE CUPS
Gladys Arndt, Fort Atkinson, Wisconsin
(Pictured at left)

One classic recipe I pull out every Yuletide is for these dreamy creamy truffle cups. They're just so festive...and the smooth filling melts as fast as snowflakes on your tongue!

  3/4 cup heavy whipping cream
    3 tablespoons butter
    1 tablespoon instant coffee granules
2-2/3 cups milk chocolate chips
2-2/3 cups red, green *or* white candy coating disks
Red and green sprinkles

In a saucepan, heat cream and butter over medium heat until bubbles form around sides of saucepan (mixture should reach a temperature of 180°). Remove from the heat; whisk in coffee granules. In a microwave-safe bowl, melt chocolate chips. Stir in cream mixture until blended. Cover and refrigerate until firm, about 2 hours.

In a microwave-safe bowl, melt candy coating disks. On a baking sheet, place 30 miniature paper or foil muffin liners. With a pastry brush, brush inside of each liner with melted candy coating. Refrigerate until set. Apply a second layer of candy coating and refrigerate until set.

Carefully peel liner away from chocolate; discard liners. Remove filling from the refrigerator; stir. If mixture is too thick, microwave at 5- to 10-second intervals until soft enough to pipe. Spoon filling into a pastry bag fitted with a large star tip. Pipe stars or rosettes into truffle cups. Cover and refrigerate. Just before serving, garnish with sprinkles. **Yield:** 2-1/2 dozen.

CINNAMON ALMOND BRITTLE
Lynette Kleinschmidt, Litchfield, Minnesota
(Pictured at left)

It simply wouldn't be Christmas at our house without this old-time favorite twist on peanut brittle. No one believes how easy it is to make...and it doesn't stick to your teeth!

    2 cups sugar
  3/4 cup light corn syrup
  1/4 cup water
    3 tablespoons butter, cubed
    2 teaspoons ground cinnamon
  1/2 teaspoon salt
    3 cups slivered almonds, toasted
1-1/2 teaspoons baking soda
    1 teaspoon vanilla extract

Butter two baking sheets and keep warm in a 200° oven. In a large saucepan, combine the sugar, corn syrup and water. Cook and stir over medium heat until a candy ther-

❄ ❄ ❄

SWEET SENSATIONS to flavor your holiday celebrations include (clockwise from top, p. 46) decadent Mocha Truffle Cups, dazzling Old-Fashioned Lollipops and crunchy Cinnamon Almond Brittle.

mometer reads 240° (soft-ball stage). Stir in the butter, cinnamon, salt and almonds; cook and stir until mixture reaches 300° (hard-crack stage), brushing down sides of pan with water as needed.

Remove from the heat; stir in baking soda and vanilla. Quickly pour onto prepared baking sheets. Spread with a buttered metal spatula to 1/4-in. thickness. Cool; break into pieces. Store in an airtight container. **Yield:** about 2 pounds.

Editor's Note: We recommend that you test your candy thermometer before each use by bringing water to a boil; the thermometer should read 212°. Adjust your recipe temperature up or down based on your test.

OLD-FASHIONED LOLLIPOPS
Penny Reifenrath, Wynot, Nebraska
(Pictured at left)

Kids of all ages will savor these fun fruity lollipops. I received the recipe from my sister-in-law years ago. We still make them in a rainbow of jewel colors in her memory every Christmas. They're great stocking stuffers!

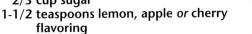

Lollipop sticks
    1 cup light corn syrup
  2/3 cup sugar
1-1/2 teaspoons lemon, apple *or* cherry
      flavoring
  1/8 teaspoon yellow, green *or* red liquid food
      coloring

Place lollipop sticks in hard candy molds or arrange sticks 3 in. apart on greased foil-lined baking sheets; set aside. In a heavy saucepan, bring corn syrup and sugar to a boil over medium heat, stirring occasionally. Cover and cook for 3 minutes to dissolve sugar crystals. Uncover and cook over medium-high heat, without stirring, until a candy thermometer reads 300° (hard-crack stage).

Remove from the heat; stir in flavoring and food coloring, keeping face away from mixture as odor is very strong. Immediately pour into prepared molds or pour free-form over ends of lollipop sticks on baking sheets; cool before removing. **Yield:** 1 dozen.

Sweeten the Trip Home

● Don't let guests leave empty-handed this holiday season. Tuck homemade goodies such as a few mints, truffles, popcorn mix or fancy cookies into squares of red and green cellophane. Tie up with pretty ribbon and place on a tray near the door. Let family and friends choose one as they leave your house.

● Or wrap up some audio books of all-time family Christmas classics such as *The Best Christmas Pageant Ever*, *A Child's Christmas in Wales* or *The Birds' Christmas Carol* to shorten the long ride home for guests.

HOLLY BUTTER MINTS
Carma Blosser, Livermore, Colorado
(Pictured above)

A merrier melt-in-your-mouth sweet than this butter-mint holly would be hard to find! It's inexpensive to make, looks so lovely on a candy tray and doesn't require refrigeration.

1/4 cup butter, softened
1/4 cup water
   1 teaspoon peppermint extract
   1 teaspoon butter flavoring
Dash salt
5-1/2 to 6 cups confectioners' sugar
Green and red gel food coloring
Granulated sugar

In a large mixing bowl, cream butter. Gradually add the water, peppermint extract, butter flavoring and salt. Beat in enough confectioners' sugar on medium speed until dough achieves a stiff putty consistency, about 3 minutes. Divide dough into three portions. Knead green food coloring into two portions. Knead red food coloring into remaining portion.

For holly leaves, shape teaspoonfuls of green dough into balls; roll in granulated sugar. Flatten to 1/8-in. thickness; cut with a holly leaf cookie cutter. For holly berries, shape 1/4 teaspoonfuls of red dough into balls; roll in granulated sugar. Arrange leaves and berries on a serving platter. Store at room temperature. **Yield:** about 12 dozen (1-3/4 pounds).

JELLIED CRANBERRY-NUT CANDIES
Linda Edwards, Elkhorn, Wisconsin

Even before they've licked the last bit of sugar off their fingers, folks are asking for more of this blue-ribbon candy. It took first place at the county fair, and everyone's sweet on these pretty squares.

   1 teaspoon butter
   1 can (16 ounces) jellied cranberry sauce

1-3/4 cups sugar, *divided*
   2 packages (3 ounces *each*) lemon gelatin
   1 package (3 ounces) orange gelatin
1-1/2 cups chopped walnuts

Line an 8-in. square pan with foil and grease the foil with 1 teaspoon butter; set aside. In a large saucepan, combine the cranberry sauce, 1 cup sugar, and lemon and orange gelatin. Bring to a boil over medium heat, stirring constantly. Remove from the heat; stir in walnuts. Pour into prepared pan. Cover and refrigerate overnight.

Using foil, lift candy out of pan; discard foil. Cut into 1-in. squares. Roll in remaining sugar. Store at room temperature between layers of waxed paper in an airtight container. Candy is best made at least 4 days before serving. **Yield:** 2-1/2 pounds.

CRUNCHY PEANUT BUTTER SQUARES
Betty Lemke, Tucson, Arizona

I've been making this candy for more than 30 years, and the first time my husband tasted it, he simply called it "the good stuff"! We've loved it each holiday ever since.

   1 teaspoon butter
   5 cups cornflakes
   1 package (10 ounces) peanut butter chips
   1 cup light corn syrup
1/2 cup sugar
1/2 cup packed brown sugar
1-3/4 cups creamy peanut butter, warmed
   1 cup dry roasted peanuts
   9 milk chocolate candy bars (1.55 ounces *each*)

Line a 13-in. x 9-in. x 2-in. baking pan with foil and grease the foil with 1 teaspoon butter; set aside. Place cornflakes in a large bowl; set aside. In a microwave, melt peanut butter chips; stir until smooth. Spread into prepared pan.

In a small saucepan, combine the corn syrup and sugars. Bring to a boil over medium heat, stirring constantly. Remove from the heat; stir in peanut butter until smooth. Stir in peanuts. Immediately pour over cornflakes; fold to combine. Spread into pan. Top with chocolate bars.

Bake at 350° for 2-4 minutes or until chocolate is melted; spread evenly. Refrigerate for up to 30 minutes or until firm. Using foil, lift candy out of pan; discard foil. Cut into 1-in. squares. Store in an airtight container. **Yield:** about 4 pounds.

WALNUT BUTTER CRUNCH
Doreen Hodges, Gilford, New Hampshire

Maybe it's the extra butter that makes this lip-smacking crunch so delectable. It takes a long time to make, but my family and friends insist it's worth every minute!

1-1/2 teaspoons plus 2 cups butter, *divided*
   2 cups sugar
1/4 cup water
   2 tablespoons light corn syrup
   2 cups coarsely chopped walnuts
TOPPING:
   1 cup (6 ounces) semisweet chocolate chips
1/2 cup finely chopped walnuts

Grease a 15-in. x 10-in. x 1-in. pan with 1-1/2 teaspoons butter; set aside. In a heavy saucepan, combine the sugar, water and corn syrup. Bring to a boil over medium heat, stirring constantly. Cube remaining butter; add to sugar mixture. Cook until a candy thermometer reads 300° (hard-crack stage). Stir in walnuts. Immediately spread into prepared pan. Cool.

In a microwave, melt chocolate chips; stir until smooth. Drizzle or spread over candy. Sprinkle with finely chopped walnuts. Break into pieces. **Yield:** about 2-1/2 pounds.

Editor's Note: We recommend that you test your candy thermometer before each use by bringing water to a boil; the thermometer should read 212°. Adjust your recipe temperature up or down based on your test.

COCONUT SNOWBALLS
Louise Irby, Gretna, Virginia

Some special recipes go from being seasonal favorites to family traditions. This is one at our house. My whole family looks forward every Christmas to these rich, once-a-year sweets.

   1 package (12 ounces) vanilla wafer crumbs, crushed
1/4 cup butter, melted
3/4 cup confectioners' sugar
   1 cup chopped pecans *or* walnuts
1/2 cup Dr. Pepper soda
ICING:
   2 cups confectioners' sugar
   2 tablespoons butter, melted
1/3 cup Dr. Pepper soda
1/4 teaspoon vanilla extract
   1 package (10 ounces) flaked coconut, toasted

In a large bowl, combine the first five ingredients. Roll into 3/4-in. balls. For icing, in a large mixing bowl, combine the confectioners' sugar, butter, soda and vanilla; beat until smooth. Dip balls in icing; shake off excess. Roll in coconut. Place on waxed paper; let stand until set. Store in an airtight container. **Yield:** about 5 dozen.

LEMON CREAM BONBONS
Ann Barber, Creola, Ohio

I used to save these special treats just for Christmastime. But they're so easy and in such demand with my family that I now keep them on hand all year-round. As pretty as sugarplums, they make lovely gifts, too.

   2 packages (8 ounces *each*) cream cheese, softened
   3 tablespoons lemon juice
   2 tablespoons grated lemon peel
   1 teaspoon lemon extract
   1 cup confectioners' sugar
   1 pound dark chocolate candy coating, chopped
1/4 pound white candy coating, chopped

In a large mixing bowl, beat the cream cheese, lemon juice, peel and extract. Gradually beat in confectioners' sugar. Cover and freeze for 2 hours.

Using a small ice cream scoop, drop mixture by 1-in. balls onto waxed paper-lined baking sheets. Cover and freeze for

1 hour. Let stand at room temperature for 10 minutes.

In a microwave, melt chocolate candy coating. Dip balls into chocolate and place on waxed paper-lined baking sheets. Let stand until set. Melt white candy coating; spoon into a heavy-duty resealable plastic bag. Cut a small hole in a corner of bag; drizzle over candies. Store in the refrigerator. **Yield:** about 4 dozen.

BLACK CHERRY SWIRL FUDGE
Paulette Bushnell, Lebanon, Oregon
(Pictured above)

This colorful treat is sure to satisfy the sweetest tooth in any family! It's always been a favorite with my nine kids, eight grandkids and my Bible study group. I even vary the soft-drink flavors to match other holidays during the year.

1-1/2 teaspoons plus 3/4 cup butter, *divided*
   3 cups sugar
3/4 cup heavy whipping cream
   1 package (10 to 12 ounces) vanilla *or* white chips
   1 jar (7 ounces) marshmallow creme
   2 envelopes unsweetened black cherry soft drink mix

Line a 13-in. x 9-in. x 2-in. pan with foil and grease the foil with 1-1/2 teaspoons butter; set aside. In a heavy saucepan, combine the sugar, cream and remaining butter. Bring to a boil over medium heat, stirring constantly. Cook and stir for 4 minutes.

Remove from the heat; stir in vanilla chips and marshmallow creme. Pour 1 cup into a bowl; set aside. Stir black cherry drink mix into the remaining marshmallow mixture. Pour into prepared pan. Spoon reserved marshmallow mixture over top; cut through mixture with a knife to swirl.

Refrigerate for 1 hour or until firm. Using foil, lift fudge out of pan; discard foil. Cut into 1-in. squares. Store in an airtight container in the refrigerator. **Yield:** about 3 pounds.

Stained Glass Cookies

Frosting Tips

- Decorate cookies like a pro with decorating tips and pastry or resealable plastic bags. Cut a small hole in the corner of the bag and insert a decorating tip. Reinforce the seal between the bag and tip with tape.

  For very simple decorations or outlining, just cut the corner off a heavy-duty resealable plastic bag.

- To fill a pastry or resealable plastic bag with frosting, insert a decorating tip if desired and place the bag in a measuring cup. Roll down top edge to make a cuff. Fill about half full with frosting. Roll up cuff.

  Smooth filling down toward tip to remove air bubbles, which will cause breaks in the design when piping. Twist top of bag shut.

Sweeten Holidays with Jeweled Ornaments

BRING BACK SWEET memories of the magic of Christmases past for your family and friends with these fancy jewel-colored cookie ornaments created especially for you by the *Country Woman* Test Kitchen.

Pretty enough to hang on a Christmas tree or up against a frosted window where they can catch the light, these cookies are certain to take your guests' breath away!

Or you might display them on a stand, as shown in photo at left, in the center of your Christmas table for a showstopping holiday centerpiece.

You can make the cookies in a variety of seasonal shapes and sizes, then add melted hard-candy centers and a creamy icing for extra detail.

(We experimented with both Lifesavers and Jolly Rancher candies, and found that the Jolly Ranchers provided a much more translucent and shiny-looking center.)

Best of all, these colorful stunners are much easier to make than you might imagine. They could even become a fun family project or tradition.

You'll find the Test Kitchen's easy-to-follow instructions included here, with handy tips on everything from crushing the hard candy to applying the frosting, as well as how-to photos below.

So bake a batch of beautiful trims (or quick gifts) with these fancy and fanciful cookie ornaments.

STAINED GLASS COOKIE ORNAMENTS

1-1/2 cups butter, softened
1-1/2 cups sugar
   2 eggs
   3 teaspoons vanilla extract
4-1/2 cups all-purpose flour
   1 teaspoon baking soda
   1 teaspoon cream of tartar
   1 teaspoon salt
Assorted colors of Jolly Rancher
   hard candies
   1 tablespoon meringue
     powder
   3 tablespoons plus 1/2
     teaspoon water
2-2/3 cups confectioners' sugar

In a large mixing bowl, cream butter and sugar. Add eggs, one at a time, beating well after each addition. Beat in vanilla. Combine the flour, baking soda, cream of tartar and salt; gradually add to creamed mixture. Divide dough into three portions; cover and refrigerate for 30 minutes or until easy to handle.

Line baking sheets with foil and grease the foil; set aside. On a lightly floured surface, roll out one portion of dough to 1/4-in. thickness. Cut with floured 2-1/2-in. ornament-shaped cookie cutters. Cut out centers with a floured 1/2-in. cookie cutter. Place larger cutouts 2 in. apart on prepared baking sheets. Using a plastic straw, poke a small hole near the top of each cookie for hanging. Repeat with remaining dough. Reroll small cutouts if desired.

Place the same color of hard candies in small resealable plastic bags; crush candies. Sprinkle in center of cookies. Bake at 350° for 8-10 minutes or until lightly browned. Use straw to reopen hanging holes. Cool for 2-3 minutes or until candies are set before carefully removing to wire racks.

For icing, in a small mixing bowl, beat meringue powder and water until soft peaks form. Gradually beat in confectioners' sugar. Decorate cookies; let dry. Thread string through holes to hang cookies. **Yield:** about 7 dozen.

Editor's Note: To order meringue powder from Wilton Industries, Inc., call 1-800/794-5866 or visit their Web site, *www.wilton.com.*

TO ORDER the Ornament Tree in photo at left by mail, send payment of $19.99 (plus $3.95 shipping and handling for one, $4.50 for two or more) to Country Store, **Suite 7657,** P.O. Box 990, Greendale WI 53129-0990.

To order with a credit card, call toll-free **1-800/558-1013.** Or you can order on-line at *www.countrystore catalog.com.* Either way, refer to Suite 7657. Please be sure to specify item 27145 for the Ornament Tree.

Wisconsin residents, add 5% sales tax. Orders from outside the United States, please pay in U.S. funds only.

CUTTING. Cut out the centers of the cookies using mini cookie cutters in shapes similar or different to those of the larger cutouts.

CRUSHING. Place hard candies in heavy resealable plastic bag. Close bag tightly. Using a meat mallet, pound candy until finely crushed.

COLORING. With the cookies on foil-lined baking sheets, carefully sprinkle a small spoonful of crushed candy to fill center of each cutout.

A Christmas to Remember

By Carol L. Duff of Lynchburg, Virginia

"I'M SO DISAPPOINTED, Mom, I cried all night," Amanda was explaining. "Brian can't get enough time off for us to come home. And I *so* wanted the girls to have a real Christmas."

Beth gripped the telephone receiver as she blinked hard. "The girls will enjoy Christmas just as much there."

"But what about *me*? I can't go with you and Daddy to cut the tree. And what about my chocolate mint cookies?"

"I'll send you the recipe so you can start your own tradition, Amanda."

"We only have an artificial tree, Mom. An artificial tree for an artificial Christmas."

Beth had looked forward all year to having Amanda's family home for Christmas. After all, they had a tradition to keep.

It had begun that first year Beth moved to the farm as a young bride. John had taken her hand, led her past the barn and through the back pasture where, he'd said, the prettiest pine she'd ever seen just waited to be their Christmas tree.

He'd been like a kid, making her close her eyes, then announcing, "Open them now. See, there it is…our first Christmas tree!"

She hadn't had the heart to point out the crooked trunk or the gaping hole in one side. And he'd wrapped his arm around her waist as they dragged the little tree home. It had been the same every year since.

But now with Amanda unable to come home and Todd on active duty, Beth seemed to have lost all desire to participate in Christmas herself.

The next day when John announced he'd found their tree, Beth suggested, "Maybe it's time to buy an artificial tree. Get rid of all those pine needles in the carpet. Less mess to clean up, don't you think?"

John stared at her for a long moment. "Maybe you're right. It's not the tree that makes Christmas anyway."

But when Beth handed her credit card to the clerk to pay for the fake tree with lights already on it, she felt like a traitor. She couldn't bring herself to hang her treasured family ornaments on the artificial tree. So she set it in the den, plugged it in and walked away.

Over the next 2 weeks, Beth gave little thought to Christmas. If she'd gone by her feelings, it could have been July instead of December 23.

"How about some of your cookies

for dessert?," John asked after supper.

"Do you know how much cholesterol those things have?" Beth answered. "I decided not to make them this year."

"Hmmm," was all John said, reaching for his jacket and heading out the door. Within minutes, he was back.

"Look, I haven't cut our tree without you in 27 years and I'm not about to start now," he said, handing Beth a coat and pushing her out the door.

"Wait…I need gloves," she said.

Down Memory Lane

John wrapped his hand around hers and stuck it in his jacket pocket. It had been a long time since they'd held hands, and she noticed his rough skin, callused from years of hard work. But his grip was familiar and their strides matched perfectly as they followed the flashlight beam to the back pasture.

"You realize this is only the third time we've done this?," John asked.

"We've done it for 27 years."

"Just the two of us, I mean. Then the kids were born and spoiled the fun …then grandkids. I've missed being alone with my bride."

Beth stole a glance at his face.

"Close your eyes," he said.

"No! It's pitch dark and I can't see two steps in front of me."

"See? That little tree's been waiting all year for this. We couldn't disappoint him on Christmas."

Beth held the light and watched John as he chopped. She studied the deep lines around his mouth and noticed the thinning spot in his hair, the way he breathed harder than he used to. She'd always thought of John as the same young man she'd married. Somehow, time had sneaked in when she wasn't looking and left its mark. She'd been too preoccupied with children and work and worry to notice.

John turned to her with a boyish grin. "Whaddaya say we get this baby home and dress him up."

Back home, Beth made spiced orange tea as John put the lights on the tree. Together they unwrapped the ornaments…memories tucked in tissue paper and stored in a cardboard box.

There was a faded green ball from the set of 12 they'd bought at Sears their first year; a Popsicle-stick frame with a picture of 6-year-old Amanda inside, and the toy car Todd had hung when he was 4.

Their scrubby little pine was soon laden with love and memories she and John had created. And to think this year she'd almost missed it.

"There's a message on the machine," John called to Beth from the kitchen. He pushed the button and Amanda's voice poured out.

"Hey, where are you guys? Not out this late, I'm sure. Anyway, one of Brian's co-workers switched schedules with him. He has 3 extra days off! We're getting in the car now and should be there before noon tomorrow. I can't wait to smell the tree and eat a dozen cookies. See you then. Love you."

"Well," John said, "looks like you'll have a real Christmas after all."

Beth wrapped her arms around him. "I've already had my Christmas. The best one yet."

Make Christmas Sparkle with a Touch of Glass

TOO BUSY dashing through malls and last-minute to-do lists to think about holiday table trims? Not to worry!

These quick centerpiece ideas lend a feeling of Christmas to any occasion. They don't take time or money you don't have…just a simple touch of glass.

Begin by setting out some favorite glass pieces where they can catch the holiday lights. Then haul out the holly, trims and imagination to create sparkling table toppers in a twinkling!

Hosting a gala dinner for family and friends? Red and white tea roses, covered (inset at right) or uncovered, crown a cake stand in dazzling holiday style.

Here's how: Place wet floral foam on top of cake stand. Cut rose stems to 3 inches. Insert stems into foam, covering entire surface. Fill spaces with greenery. Add luster with tiny gold gift boxes and a swirl of mini lights and gold mesh.

Or welcome guests with a merry trio of ruby goblets a-shine with quiet candlelight and tucked in holly sprays.

Brighten any buffet with a hurricane vase wreathed in colorful berries and studded with sparkly red and green pears. (See our cover for yet another option.) Fill with a pillar candle and potpourri or cranberries and popcorn to convey: It's clearly Christmas! ❄

TAKE THE CAKE for easy elegance with the simple but stunning display above. We bought fresh tea roses to blossom on a cake stand amid drifts of sparkly mini lights and golden mesh fabric.

MAKE THE SEASON BRIGHT with a merry trio of chunky cranberry goblets swaddled in sprigs of holly or other fresh greens. Provide friends and family with an interesting twist on the usual tea or vigil lights by using candle balls!

BOWL THEM OVER with this festive fruited centerpiece built around a footed hurricane vase. A mirror base helps magnify the rich colors, warm candlelight and cheery glow for guests.

Frosty Fellows Warm Up Her Christmas Kitchen

By Nancy Coffey of Plano, Texas

SNOWMEN and Santas brighten Nancy's home and heart for the holiday season. "I always smile when I see one," she says. "Don't you?"

A WREATH in every window...a tree in every room...and a jolly kitchen decked from floor to ceiling in a flurry of frosty snowmen. That pretty much sums up holiday decorating at our house in Plano, Texas.

White Christmases are something folks only dream about in this suburb of Dallas. Maybe that's one reason friends and family always seem to drift in to our kitchen to chat or visit. It's simply snowed under with happy holiday spirit...and snowmen!

I've been collecting the wintry whimsical characters ever since we bought our newly built home 14 years ago. And come Christmas, they're nestled in every nook and cozied into every cranny of my "North Pole" kitchen.

Actually, it was the kitchen that first sold me on this model house, and it's been the heart of our home ever since.

Its size and many windows give the room an open, airy "country feeling" and bring in the outdoor vistas and morning sunlight even on cold wintry days.

Now that our two children are grown, my husband, Michael, and I love to share a cup of cocoa or quick meal at the table in front of our big bay windows, just watching birds and wildlife outside in the trees. The white beadboard wainscoting we recently added under those windows makes the kitchen even brighter.

Snowmen by the Sleighful

For most of the year, colonial blue curtains accent the warm almond tones of the ceramic tile floor and pale mauve checks of our wallpaper. But for the holiday season, we replace those window trims with navy blue valances sprinkled with roly-poly snowmen (a Christmas gift from a good friend). Snowmen also dance across my blue china holiday dishes and mugs—and even cover the backs of my kitchen chairs!

There are snowmen on oven mitts, teapots, fingertip towels, rugs and stovetop covers. They straddle the tops of our golden oak cabinets wreathed in evergreen garlands, sit on every sill and shelf, cuddle in couples on countertops, huddle in a sweatered set on top of the fridge, dangle in front of windows, perch on wreaths and swing from the ♂

A WINTRY WONDERLAND of snowmen, penguins and polar bears showcases Nancy's collectibles and crafting ability and sets a "North Pole" theme for her kitchen. "I buy a lot of things on sale the day after Christmas," she says. "A good friend made the Frosty-figured curtains and chair-back covers (opposite) as a gift, and I whipped up the chandelier trim and hanging baskets in the dining room with crystal icicles and ribbons."

branches of our glittery snowman tree.

On the counter space behind my kitchen sink, a tiny set of illuminated porcelain igloos nestles in cotton batting snow along with more snowmen, penguins and polar bears. At night, it all twinkles like a winter wonderland in the dark windows.

I have boxes and boxes of snowmen—at least 150 different ones. Just like my friends, they come in all sizes and sorts—wood, resin, porcelain, patchwork, plush and papier-mache, fabric, crystal, almost anything you can think of.

I can't look at a snowman and not smile—no matter how badly my day is going. Whether purchased by me or received as a gift from family or good friends, each frosty figure has its own story, memories and place in my heart. And in my kitchen!

And believe me, no one can warm a heart or a holiday welcome like these frosty fellows. That's important to Michael and me because we love holiday entertaining. For the last 20 years, we've hosted a Christmas Open House on the first Saturday of December.

Holiday Hospitality

On that gala day, this kitchen just overflows with about 150 of our friends and neighbors—as well as delectable

TUCKED IN behind the sink between two corner windows, a tiny Debbie Mumm village of lighted porcelain igloos, playful penguins and more snowmen nestles in drifts of cotton batting "snow".

desserts, fancy finger foods, festive punches, hors d'oeuvres and at least 35 different cookies and bars.

I do all the baking Thanksgiving week—and I get many of my recipes from *Country Woman* and *Taste of Home* magazines. It's a lot of work, but so much fun! And that's when I really appreciate my handy work island with

its extra counter and hidden storage space.

Our friends start talking about this event as early as summer, and it has come to mark the official start of holiday festivities for many of them. But not for us.

Michael and I start right after Halloween, working weekends and nights to get all our snowmen and other decorations put up.

We have a tree in every room—including the laundry room—10 in all! Not every one is full size, but each has its own theme...snowmen for the kitchen tree, Santas for the family room, crystal and blue ornaments for the more formal living room, patriotic for the bedroom, etc.

And, of course, decorating spills over to the exterior of the house with strings of lights, wreaths and wood cutouts of Santa and his reindeer that we made.

We've always been Christmas fanatics at our house. It's such a wonderful time of the year! People seem so much more friendly with each other ...so much more open and kind.

And somehow, even after all our trees and tinsel and snowmen are put away, that Merry Christmas spirit has a way of lingering in this kitchen all year long. It's the happiest room in our house. I hope your holidays—and home—are merry and bright for this Yuletide season!

SEASON'S GREETINGS from a caroling crowd of wood cutouts made by Nancy and her husband.

Give Kids Something to Celebrate!

SET SPIRITS STIRRING with a sleighful of festive kid-crafted table trims…and share the joys of entertaining Christmas-style with your children.

TINY TOTS with their eyes all aglow… can have such a hard time waiting for Santa to make his annual appearance.

Why not rein in some of their energy, excitement and creativity by helping them make table decorations for their very own "We Love Santa" party—then invite friends or family members?

Using paper cups, colored paper, pipe cleaners or chenille stems, scissors and glue, you can give youngsters a taste of the fun that comes with crafting a Christmas surprise for others.

In the process, you'll be sharing some merry moments together—and creating memories to last a lifetime.

Begin by using paper tablecloths, cups and plates in holiday colors to eliminate all worry about spills or broken dishes.

Even very young children can help glue precut strips of red and green paper into paper chains. They can hang these with cellophane tape around the party room or table.

Older children will want to try the festive Santa garland in the photo above.

Using a craft knife, have an adult cut a small X in the bottom of eight red plastic-coated paper cups. Give the children white chenille stems to form individual letters that spell out "We" and "Santa" and to make a small heart shape.

Attach the letters and heart to inverted paper cups with narrow strips of double-stick tape. Use a pushpin to pierce random holes through the sides of each paper cup.

Attach an artificial evergreen garland to the table edge. String white mini lights around garland. Slip paper cups over exposed lights (as shown in photo above) to spell out a warm twinkling welcome to the guest of honor!

Paper cups also make thrifty nifty party favors. Use a scissors to remove 1 inch from the top of each cup. Cut a small slit into opposite sides of each cup about 1/2 inch from edge. Attach a white chenille stem for a hanger.

Wrap another white chenille stem around top of rim. Glue as needed to hold. Add gummed white letters to each cup to spell out guests' first names (see photo at right). Fill to brimming with jolly treats and set at each place or hang from each guest's chair.

Encourage the kids to exchange small gifts or a favorite slightly used book or toy. Make gift tags by tracing Christmas cookie cutters on construction paper. Cut out and label each with a guest's name. (Older kids can outline each shape with glue, then sprinkle on glitter for added sparkle.)

So crank up the carols and share the jolly spirit of this giving season with your children! ❅

PARTY-PRETTY paper cup favors double as place markers and are easy and economical.

Grandma's Angels...

LOOK WHAT SANTA BROUGHT! Shelby Hochstein, 2-1/2, couldn't *be* happier or more excited with new baby sister Sonya, chuckles Great-Grandma Delma Snyder in McCook, Nebraska.

LO AND BEHOLD! Grandbaby Morgan came as a happy Christmas surprise, nestled all snug in Grandma Harriet Roth's holiday stocking, she notes from her home in Bradenton, Florida.

A-CAROLING WE GO. Santa's sidekicks Will, Jared and Nathan Cushlanis sing for Grandma Myra Hattrich. "They make my Yuletide merry and bright," she writes from Sparta, North Carolina.

AWAY IN A MANGER, grandkids Jackson, 2, Hannah, 4, and baby Ethan find the reason to celebrate, acting out the first Christmas for Lois VanDerwerken in Schoharie, New York.

ANGEL BABY is the nickname her smile and her wings earned adorable 1-year-old Noelle Page. Proud Grandma Carol Gibson from Martin, Tennessee snapped the cute holiday photo.

SITTING PRETTY and poised in a patch of poinsettias is redheaded Miranda Mathiason. "She's a real Christmas joy!" exclaims her great-grandma Marie Wood of Granada, Minnesota.

Echoes of Christmas Past Bring Home Resounding Joy

By Penny J. Martin of Hanover, Pennsylvania

THE DAY began like any other. I filled the coffeepot at the kitchen sink and stared out the window at the rolling fields behind our farmhouse.

But this wasn't just any day. It was Christmas morning, and the fields once barren were blanketed with snow. Carols on the radio were suddenly interrupted by a weather report stating this was the first white Christmas in 25 years.

My mind drifted back in time. Twenty-five years ago, I was rocking 9-day-old Jason by the Christmas tree. Now he was a grown man with his own tree and a 2-year-old daughter, Emily.

I gazed over at the staircase, half expecting to hear the clamor of three pairs of tiny feet racing down the stairs to see what Santa had left them. My heart ached, knowing I would never hear that joyful sound again.

My daughter, Jess, was celebrating her first Christmas with her new husband. And 16-year-old Brian was upstairs still sound asleep. I doubted if even the hooves of eight reindeer on the roof would wake him this early.

Life was changing. For the first time in as many years as I'd been married to Howard, we weren't going to Grandmom's house for Christmas Day. Now *my* grandchild was coming to *her* grandmother's house for Christmas.

Staring out at the relentless snowfall, I prayed silently: *Please let them make it home safely.*

My prayers were quickly answered when the door opened and a beautiful snow-covered angel appeared.

"Jess!" I ran to her with open arms. "Merry Christmas!"

I watched contentment fill my husband's face as he hugged our only daughter. Had he, too, been feeling the changes?

Brian finally awoke to join us. At least I still had one pair of not-so-tiny feet clamoring down the steps.

Soon Jason and Darlene arrived with a tiny pink marshmallow in tow. Was that Emily under the puffy snowsuit?

She ran over to me, "Mom-Mom!"

I fell to my knees and hugged her to my heart. "Merry Christmas, Emily."

Jason shouted from the next room, "Is breakfast ready?"

I looked toward the living room, brimming with Christmas packages. "Don't you want to open presents first?"

"No!" All my children shouted in unison.

Another change. It didn't seem that long ago they were knocking on our bedroom door at 6 a.m., begging to open gifts.

When we finally did get around to the presents, I watched anxiously as each one of my children ripped into a package. *Does he like it? Is that the color she wanted? Is that the size he asked for?* Some things never change.

The snow continued to fall, but I no longer worried. My family was safe in the warmth of their home. And then it dawned on me: No matter where they went or how far they traveled, this would always be their home.

The home we had created in this old farmhouse, the same one I'd cursed for being too small to hold a family of five and two dogs, was now a haven. A haven for the family my husband and I had created. A family that would continue to grow long after we were gone.

Changes, I thought wryly, remembering my old dream of an addition on the side of the house. *We'll have to make it bigger now for all the grandchildren who will be coming.* I smiled at Howard and he smiled back. He obviously didn't know what I was thinking.

Yes, life is full of changes. I'll always miss those days when my children were little…but what sweet memories I have.

And smiling down at my granddaughter, I thought of all the wonderful memories I still had to look forward to. Maybe changes weren't so bad, after all. ❄

Meet Our Artist...

Her Whimsical Creations Celebrate The Childlike Wonder of Christmas

In the following interview, she shares with us a glimpse of her warmhearted whimsical world.

Q. How did you get started in your line of work?

A. *From the age of 3, I've had a fascination with trying to put the ideas in my head on paper with paints or any other art media I could find.*

Growing up in a large Puerto Rican family of nine children, we found imaginative ways to enrich our lives. I'm sure our creativity was passed down to us by our parents. Both were artistic in their own right and inspired us early on.

My father had a deep love of music and would sing and play wonderful Spanish ballads for us on his guitar. My mother loved to sew and was a thrifty and ingenious seamstress. With six girls to clothe, she often made six versions of the same dress from the same fabric. I can still remember people asking her if we were a singing group!

After high school, I went on to study graphic design, but watercolor painting and crafting remain creative outlets.

Q. How do you decorate your own home for the holidays?

A. *Christmas is my favorite time of year, and I like to deck my rooms from floor to ceiling with garlands, scented candles and old-time collectibles. I've collected holiday trims for years, and each has great sentimental value to me.*

I also enjoy making my own decorations and giving them as gifts to friends and family—or even selling them. Over

EMMA ACEVEDO joined Reiman Publications in 1999.

She is Art Director for its flagship food magazine, *Taste of Home*, and also for the annual *Country Woman Christmas* book... and adds her unique artistic touch and skillful designs to both publications.

CHRISTMAS NEVER FAILS to bring out the creative spirit in artist Emma Acevedo. She crafts holiday gift items and cards and decks her home in a sleighful of handmade seasonal trims.

the years, I've created items that have been inspired by my illustrations (left)… things like fabric dolls, keepsake boxes for all seasons, greeting cards and picture frames.

Q. What's a favorite holiday film?
A. *I love "It's a Wonderful Life" with Jimmy Stewart. My grandfather was a lot like him in that movie…always standing up for the little guy and for what he believed was right.*

Q. How do you fill your free time?
A. *I take walks, shop flea markets and care for my pet rabbit. I also own a home-based craft business, Small Talks.*

I really love snowmen and have a collection that grows bigger every year. This year I made my own family of them (right), crafting the resin models from molds made from my original papier-mache sculptures.

Through my art, I try to convey what I feel is missing in the world today, that age of innocence when we all heard jingle bells on the roof while pretending to be asleep. It's the magic of those memories—that kind of wonder—that I want to rub off on people when they view my creations. ❄

WATCHING FOR THE CHRISTMAS STAR. Emma's frosty folks are signed resin copies of her own original papier-mache art. Each heirloom-quality figure is stained, painted and glittered by hand with such added whimsical touches as wire glasses, earmuffs and hand-fringed wool scarfs.

Try These Creative Greetings!

EVEN if your family isn't as large as Emma's, you're likely to have a box full of photographic memories hidden away somewhere in a closet or drawer just waiting to be used in a fun craft project.

Here Emma shares an idea for using old or recent photos to add a personal touch to your holiday greetings. "And it's less expensive than store-bought cards," she notes.

Start with blank folded card stock. Cut a piece of colored paper to fit the front of the folded card and glue it onto the card. Glue a favorite snapshot in the center of the colored paper. You could also cut a window in the colored paper to use as a frame for your photo.

Then add your choice of trims. "For the sample card at lower right, I cut shapes from white paper and added stripes with a red marker to make them look like holiday candies," explains Emma.

"Artificial holiday trims are another option for decorating your cards (see top left sample). I twisted two different trims together and glued them to one side of the card.

"Sometimes I wrap ribbon around the top of a card and glue a bow of the same ribbon in the center. Or I might add snowflake stickers to an outdoor photo."

Finally, a magnetic strip glued to the back of the cards turns them into memorable refrigerator keepsakes. "The options are as endless," says Emma, "as your imagination!"

Craft Section

Cherish Holiday Memories with Keepsake Album

IT'S A SNAP to preserve precious memories of Christmases past with this adorable miniature photo album from Amy Burks.

"These little books go together in no time at all with just a glue gun, scrap snippets, a twist of raffia and touch of greenery," says the Midland, Michigan crafter.

And what a merry gift idea for teachers, friends or far-flung family members!

Materials Needed:

Photo album (4-inch x 6-inch photo size)
10-1/2-inch x 16-1/2-inch piece of red plaid fabric or size needed to cover photo album
4-inch x 5-inch piece of natural burlap
Pinking shears
Straight scissors
Four 1-inch-long miniature spring clothespins
Two 4-inch-long sprigs of snow-tipped artificial evergreen
Two 5-inch-long red berry sprigs
Two 1-inch-long pinecones
Small flat paintbrush
Textured snow medium
Four 12-inch-long strands of natural raffia
Ruler or measuring tape
White (tacky) glue

Finished Size: Pinecone photo album measures 5 inches wide x 6-1/2 inches high x 2-1/2 inches deep.

Directions:

Use paintbrush to apply textured snow medium to tips of each pinecone. Let dry.

Using pinking shears, trim 1/4 in. from all sides of the 10-1/2-in. x 16-1/2-in. piece of red plaid fabric.

Place red plaid fabric wrong side up on a flat surface. Center opened photo album on top of fabric.

Referring to Fig. 1 below, use straight scissors to trim excess fabric from top and bottom edges of photo album spine as shown.

Fold and glue the remaining 1/4-in. edge of fabric to the top and bottom edges of the spine. Then fold and glue the top, bottom and side edges of fabric to inside front and back covers, completely covering the outside of the photo album. Let dry.

Using pinking shears, trim 1/4 in. from all edges of the 4-in. x 5-in. piece of burlap.

Refer to the photo above as a guide while assembling cover as directed in the instructions that follow.

Clip a mini clothespin onto each corner of the burlap piece.

Center burlap piece on front cover of photo album. Glue burlap and clothespins right side up to front cover. Let dry.

Glue berry and evergreen sprigs to the burlap piece. Let dry.

Working with all strands of raffia as one, tie raffia in a bow. Trim ends as desired. Glue bow to bottom of berry and pine sprigs. Let dry.

Glue pinecones to center of raffia bow. Let dry. Tuck your favorite holiday photos inside! ★

Fig. 1 Cutting album fabric

Cut
1/4 in.
Front cover | Spine of photo album | Back cover
1/4 in.
Cut

Picture This!

Saving photos in small albums based on specific holidays is a great way to start organizing those boxes and bags full of loose snapshots most families treasure but seldom see.

Folks love paging through memories of Christmases past each holiday season to compare trees, decorations, gifts and gatherings. It's easy to update and always fun to see how family and friends have grown and changed over the years!

Jolly Jar Is Decked in Frosty Finery

TRIMMED IN holiday style, this thrifty gift jar with its snowman necklace makes a pretty and practical salute to the season.

Says crafter Lenora Schut of Pella, Iowa, "It's a big seller at Christmas bazaars and a quick and easy way to dress up Yuletide gifts of candy, nuts or hot cocoa mix."

Materials Needed:

Purchased wooden cutouts—
  2-1/2-inch-high split snowman, two 1-1/4-inch-high x 3/16-inch-thick mittens, two 1-inch-high x 1/8-inch-thick snowflakes
Nine 3/8-inch natural wooden beads
Drill with 1/8-inch bit
Finishing sandpaper
Tack cloth
Foam plate or palette
Paper towels
Water container
Acrylic craft paints (Lenora used DecoArt Americana)—Cadmium Yellow, Forest Green, Jack-O-Lantern Orange, Lamp Black, Light French Blue, Napa Red and Warm White
Paintbrushes—small flat and liner
1-inch foam brush
Toothpick
Small screw eye
1/2-inch x 4-inch torn strip of red-and-green check fabric
24-inch length of 1/16-inch-wide red satin ribbon
Clear glass jar with screw-on lid
Scissors

Finished Size: Necklace is about 24 inches long x 2-1/2 inches high.

Directions:

Referring to Fig. 1 below, drill a hole through two opposite points of each snowflake and through corners of each mitten. Sand wood pieces smooth and wipe each clean with tack cloth.

PAINTING: Keep paper towels and container of water handy to clean the brushes. Place dabs of each paint color on foam plate or palette as needed. Paint all sides of wood pieces as directed. Add coats of paint as needed for complete coverage. Let paint dry after every application.

Refer to photo at right as a guide while painting as directed in the instructions that follow.

Use flat brush and Forest Green to paint five wooden beads.

Use the flat brush and Warm White to paint all sides of each snowflake and the head and body of the snowman.

Use the flat brush and Light French Blue to paint snowman's hat.

Use the flat brush and Cadmium Yellow to paint all sides of each mitten and the narrow band on the snowman's hat.

Referring to Fig. 2 below, paint small dip-dot hearts on each side of each mitten. To paint dip-dot hearts, dip end of liner handle into Napa Red and dab on two small side-by-side dots of paint. While paint is still wet, use handle to pull paint down from each dot, creating the point of the heart.

Dip the handle end of liner into Lamp Black and dab three small dots down center front of the snowman's body for buttons. In the same way, add two smaller Lamp Black dots to snowman's head for eyes.

Use liner and Lamp Black to paint snowman's mouth.

Dip toothpick into Warm White and add a tiny dot to each eye.

Use liner and Jack-O-Lantern Or-

ange to add small triangle for nose.

Dip flat brush into Napa Red and wipe excess paint off on paper towel. With a nearly dry brush and a circular motion, add cheeks to snowman.

Use liner and Lamp Black to add stitch lines to each heart and to add a dashed outline around the edge of each side of each mitten.

Use foam brush and Napa Red to paint lid of jar. Let dry.

Screw lid on jar.

ASSEMBLY: Insert screw eye into top of snowman's hat.

Fold length of red ribbon in half. Insert fold of ribbon through screw eye. Slip ends of ribbon through loop and pull to tighten ribbon around screw eye.

Thread both ends of ribbon through one green bead.

Separate ends of ribbon and add a natural bead to each end.

Thread each ribbon end through drilled holes in each mitten, making sure the mittens face in opposite directions.

Add a green bead to each end of the ribbon.

Thread each ribbon end through drilled holes in each snowflake.

Add a green and a natural bead to each end of the ribbon.

Place the necklace around the top of the jar and tie the ribbon ends together in a small bow.

Change the necklace to match the seasons, and this jar will brighten a kitchen all year-round! ★

Fig. 1 Drilling holes

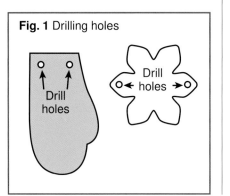

Drill holes

Drill holes

Fig. 2 Painting dip-dot hearts

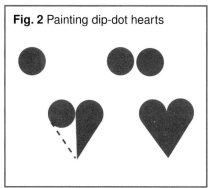

Painted Bottle Plugs Into Warmth of Season

ALL A-TWINKLE, this pretty recycled bottle from Merritt Island, Florida crafter Alise Duerr is sure to make your holidays bright!

She adds cheery candy canes, a string of mini lights and tucks her painted bottles in a corner of her kitchen counter, on a mantel or atop a table. "They make distinctive gifts but are so quick, easy and inexpensive to put together," she points out. And they brighten the season for friends.

Materials Needed:
Pattern below
Tracing paper and pencil
Graphite paper
Masking tape
Empty dark green glass bottle (see Finished Size at right)
Matte finish spray (Alise used Krylon Matte Finish Spray)
Foam plate or palette
Paper towels
Water container
Acrylic craft paints (Alise used Delta Ceramcoat)—Forest Green, Leaf Green, Light Ivory, Nightfall Blue and Opaque Red
Small piece of household sponge or sea sponge
Paintbrushes—Nos. 4 and 6 flat and script liner
Gum eraser
Clear matte spray (Alise used Krylon Crystal Clear Matte Spray)
24-inch length of 1-1/2-inch-wide red sheer ribbon
Strand of 25 white mini lights
Scissors

Finished Size: Bottle shown measures 3 inches across x 12-1/2 inches high. Pattern may be enlarged or reduced on a photocopy machine to fit larger or smaller bottles.

PAINTED BOTTLE PATTERN
Trace 1—tracing paper
Paint as directed in instructions

Directions:
Remove all labels from bottle and wash with soapy water. Let dry.

Spray outside of bottle with an even coat of matte finish, following spray manufacturer's directions. Let dry.

SPONGE PAINTING: Dampen household sponge or sea sponge piece with clean water.

Place a small amount of Light Ivory on foam plate or palette. Dip household sponge or sea sponge piece into paint Dab sponge piece on paper towel to remove excess paint.

Using an up-and-down motion, sponge-paint outside of bottle. Let dry.

PAINTING: Candy Cane: Trace the pattern at left onto tracing paper with pencil.

Referring to photo above for position, place pattern on bottle and slip graphite paper between pattern and bottle. Tape as needed to hold pattern in place.

Trace over pattern lines with a dull pencil to transfer pattern onto one side of bottle. Remove pattern and tape.

Keep paper towels and a container of water handy to clean brushes. Place dabs of each paint color on foam plate or palette as needed.

Add coats of paint as needed for

complete coverage. Let paint dry after every application.

Refer to photo and pattern as guides while painting as directed in the instructions that follow.

Use No. 6 flat brush and Light Ivory to paint each entire candy cane. Let dry.

Use No. 4 flat brush and Opaque Red to add wide stripes to each candy cane.

Use liner and Opaque Red to add narrow stripes on each candy cane.

Dip No. 4 flat brush into clean water and blot brush on paper towel until shine leaves the brush.

Dip one corner of brush into Nightfall Blue. Brush bristles back and forth on foam plate or palette to blend color and water. The color should fade from dark to light to clear.

With paint-loaded side of brush on the outside, shade the lower edges of each candy cane and the areas where the candy canes overlap.

Use liner and Light Ivory to highlight the center of each candy cane.

Pine boughs: Use liner and Forest Green to paint the branch of each pine bough.

Use liner and Forest Green to add the longer needles coming from the branch of each pine bough.

Use liner and Leaf Green to add the shorter needles coming from the branch of each pine bough.

Use liner and Light Ivory to add highlights to pine boughs.

FINISHING: Use the gum eraser to erase any pattern lines that show.

Spray outside of bottle with matte finish spray. Let dry.

Spray outside of bottle with two coats of clear matte spray, following spray manufacturer's instructions. Let dry.

Insert bulbs of mini light string into bottle, leaving plug end of cord outside the bottle so you can plug it in.

Holding cord at the back, wrap ribbon around top of bottle and over cord. Tie ribbon in a bow on front of bottle. Trim ribbon ends as desired.

Light up your Noel nights with this recycled gift idea! ✩

Cute Pins Are Cut Out For Holiday Fashion Fun

SPICE UP your holiday gift list with these adorable "gingerbread" pins from Verlyn King of Tremonton, Utah. They are scented with cinnamon, apple and nutmeg, sparkling with Christmas colors and look good enough to eat!

"I used mini cookie cutters to make Christmas shapes," Verlyn chuckles.

Materials Needed (for all):
3/4 cup applesauce
2 tablespoons white (tacky) glue
1 cup cinnamon
1 tablespoon nutmeg
Waxed paper
Rolling pin
Mini cookie cutters—1-1/4-inch star, 1-inch-long mitten, 1-1/2-inch-long candy cane and 1-1/2-inch-long gingerbread boy
Aluminum foil
Baking sheet
Acrylic craft paints—red and white
Small round paintbrush
Eight 4-inch-long pieces of artificial wired pine bough
Four 14-inch lengths of 1/8-inch-wide red satin ribbon
Eight 2-1/2-inch lengths of 3mm red metallic string beads
Four 3-inch lengths of craft wire
Glue gun and glue sticks
Four 1-inch pin backs

Finished Size: Each pin is about 2-1/2 inches long x 2 inches wide.

Directions:
Mix applesauce and glue together in a small bowl. Add cinnamon and nutmeg and mix well.

Knead ingredients together, adding more cinnamon if needed to make a stiff dough. Place dough between two pieces of waxed paper; use rolling pin to roll out dough to 1/4-in. thickness.

Use mini cookie cutters to cut out shapes. Place shapes on a foil-covered baking sheet and allow to dry, carefully turning pieces once.

When dry, paint white designs on star and mitten, and red and white details on gingerbread boy and candy cane as shown in photo above. Let dry.

Fold each length of wired pine bough in half. Glue two lengths of string beads to the center of each piece of wired pine bough.

Loop each length of ribbon back and forth to form three loops on each side of the center. Secure center of loops with a piece of craft wire. Then wire a looped ribbon to the center of each pine bough.

Glue a cookie cutter shape onto the front of each pine bough and a pin back centered onto the back of each.

Pin on your own holiday outfit…and enjoy the aroma of the season! ✩

Finger Towel Keeps St. Nick at Hand

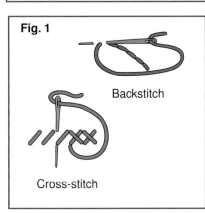

A BUNDLE OF TOYS flung over his back, this right jolly old elf will keep Christmas memories and dreams close at hand.

Crafted and cross-stitched by Penny Duff of Kennebunk, Maine, the festive fingertip towel makes a handy holiday keepsake or gift.

Materials Needed:
Chart below
14-inch x 24-inch white fringed terry cloth towel with 3-inch-wide 14-count Aida cloth insert (Penny used a Charles Craft Kitchen Mates towel)
DMC six-strand embroidery floss in colors listed on color key
Size 24 tapestry needle
Scissors

Finished Size: Design area of towel is 32 stitches high x 177 stitches wide and measures about 2-1/4 inches high x 12-3/4 inches wide.

Directions:
Fold Aida cloth insert of towel in half

lengthwise and then in half crosswise to determine center and mark this point.

To find center of towel chart, draw lines across chart, connecting opposite arrows. Begin stitching Santa at this point so design will be centered. Stitch border section on each side of Santa where shown on chart.

Working with 18-in. lengths of six-strand floss, separate strands and use three strands for cross-stitches and one strand for backstitches. See Fig. 1 below left for stitch illustrations.

Each square on chart equals one stitch worked over a set of fabric threads. Use colors indicated on color key to complete cross-stitching.

Do not knot floss on back of work. Instead, leave a tail of floss on back of work and hold it in place while working the first few stitches over it. To end a strand, run needle under a few neighboring stitches in back before cutting floss close to work.

When stitching is complete, and only if necessary, gently wash stitched towel in lukewarm water. Press right side down on another terry towel to dry.

Deck your kitchen with holiday flair!

CROSS-STITCH SANTA CHART

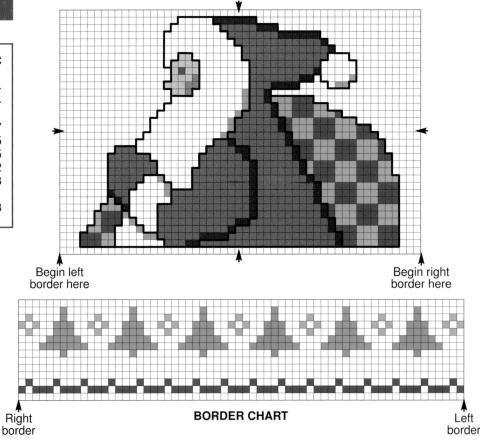

Begin left border here

Begin right border here

COLOR KEY	DMC
☐ White	
▨ Light Shell Pink	224
▨ Medium Holiday Red	304
▨ Medium Navy Blue	311
▨ Dark Pistachio Green	367
▨ Pearl Gray	415
▨ Medium Garnet	815
☐ Light Antique Blue	932
☐ Very Light Peach Flesh	948
BACKSTITCH	
▬ Very Dark Coffee Brown	898

Fig. 1

Backstitch

Cross-stitch

Right border

BORDER CHART

Left border

Old-Fashioned Fellows Are Fit to Be Tied on Trees, Gifts

CUTE, CHRISTMASY and COUNTRY, these whimsical snowmen are dressed in cheery red long johns for their "long winter's naps"! Crafted by Sandy Dye from Clarion, Pennsylvania, the clever characters will brighten any tree or gift package.

Materials Needed (for three snowmen):

Three 5-1/2-inch-long red knit long johns (see shopping information)
Polyester stuffing
Three 1-inch Styrofoam balls
Water container
Foam plate or palette
Textured snow medium (Sandy used Delta Decorative Snow)
Acrylic craft paints (Sandy used Delta Ceramcoat)—Black and Terra Cotta
Small flat paintbrush
Three round toothpicks
Rusty tin trims—one 2-inch star, one 1-inch star and four 1/2-inch jingle bells
Rusty craft wire—four 8-inch lengths and one 2-inch length
Needle-nose pliers
Wool fabric for scarves—one 1/2-inch x 8-inch strip of green-and-black plaid and two 1/2-inch x 8-inch strips of red-and-black plaid
Finishing nail and hammer
One 3-inch-long green cedar sprig
White (tacky) glue (Sandy used Crafter's Pick Ultimate Glue)
Scissors

Shopping Information: The long johns are available from Sandy Dye Long Johns, 19 S. Fifth Ave., Clarion PA 16214. Enclose $5 for each long john.

Finished Size: Excluding hangers and trims, each long john ornament measures about 3-1/2 inches across x 6-1/2 inches long.

Directions:

Use flat brush to apply textured snow medium to each Styrofoam ball. Let dry.

Break off a 1-in. length from each toothpick for noses. Paint each nose Terra Cotta. Let dry.

Stuff each long john with stuffing.

Glue a head to the neck opening of each long john. Let dry.

Glue a nose to the center front of each head. Let dry.

Dip a remaining toothpick piece into Black and use to dab two tiny dots onto each head for eyes. In the same way, add five tiny dots to each for mouths. Let dry.

Use flat brush to apply a bit of snow medium to the top of each nose. Let dry.

FINISHING: Refer to photo as a guide when assembling snowmen as directed in instructions that follow.

For hangers, insert the ends of an 8-in. length of wire into back of each snowman. Use needle-nose pliers to twist wire ends together to hold. Form each hanger into an arc.

Large star snowman: Wrap a green-and-black plaid scarf around snowman's neck and tie ends in an overhand knot in front.

Glue the 2-in. rusty star to front of snowman. Glue arms to star to hold. Let dry.

Jingle bell snowman: Place a small amount of Terra Cotta on foam plate or palette. Add clean water to thin paint to an ink-like consistency. Use paintbrush to apply thinned paint to one snowman's head to give an aged look.

Wrap a red-and-black plaid scarf around snowman's neck and tie ends in an overhand knot in front.

Thread a rusty jingle bell onto remaining 8-in. length of rusty wire. Use needle-nose pliers to twist wire about 2-1/2 in. from the end to hold the bell in place.

Add remaining jingle bells and twist wire as before, spacing the bells about 1/2 in. apart along the wire.

Insert opposite ends of wire through the ends of the snowman's arms. Use needle-nose pliers to coil wire on back of each to hold.

Evergreen snowman: Wrap a red-and-black plaid scarf around snowman's neck and tie ends in an overhand knot in front.

Use hammer and nail to make a hole through one point of the 1-in. rusty star.

Thread the 2-in. length of rusty wire through hole in star. Use needle-nose pliers to coil end of wire on front of star. Thread other end of wire through end of left arm of snowman. Use needle-nose pliers to coil end of wire on back of arm.

Glue green cedar sprig to right front of snowman. Glue arm to sprig to hold. Let dry.

Make several extras to keep on hand as quick gifts! ✫

Tree Skirt Spreads Joy of the Holidays

RINGING IN the holidays is easy with this old-fashioned crocheted tree skirt. Crafter Nanette Hankins sized it just right for circling the tiny table tree in her Old Fort, North Carolina home.

"I decorate that tree for every holiday of the year. With this skirt, I can change the color of ribbons and bows to coordinate with seasonal celebrations—whether it's Christmas, Easter, Halloween or Thanksgiving!" she writes.

Materials Needed:
16-ounces of 4-ply (heavyweight) off-white cotton crochet thread
Size G/6 (4.25mm) crochet hook or size needed to obtain correct gauge
Yarn or tapestry needle
18-inch x 44-inch piece of coordinating red plaid fabric for trim
Matching all-purpose thread
Rotary cutter and mat (optional)
Quilter's marking pen or pencil (optional)
Quilter's ruler
Eight small dressmaker snaps
Standard sewing supplies

Gauge: 4 dcs and 2 rows = 1 inch. Slight variations in gauge will change the finished size a bit.

Finished Size: Table tree skirt measures about 24 inches across.

Directions:
Row 1: Ch 42, sc in second ch from hk and in each remaining ch across, turn: 41 scs.

Row 2: Ch 5 (counts as first tr and ch-1), sk next sc, tr in next sc, [ch 1, sk next sc, tr in next sc] across, turn: 20 ch-1 sps.

Row 3: Ch 1 for first sc, sc in each tr and in each ch-1 sp across, turn: 41 scs.

Row 4: Ch 3 (counts as first dc here and throughout), dc in next sc, [work 2 dcs in next sc, dc in next 2 scs] across, turn: 54 dcs.

Row 5: Ch 3, dc in next dc, * ch 2, sk next 2 dcs, [dc in next dc, work 2 dcs in next dc] twice; repeat from * across to last 4 dcs, ch 2, sk next 2 dcs, dc in last 2 dcs, turn: 9 ch-2 sps (eyelets) and 52 dcs.

Row 6: Ch 3, dc in next dc, * work 2 dcs in next ch-2 sp, [work 2 dcs in next dc, dc in next 2 dcs] twice; repeat from * across to last ch-2 sp, work 2 dcs in last ch-2 sp, dc in last 2 dcs, turn: 86 dcs.

Row 7: Ch 3, dc in next dc, ch 2, sk next 2 dcs, [dc in next 8 dcs, ch 2, sk 2 dcs] across to last 2 dcs, dc in last 2 dcs, turn: 9 ch-2 sps and 68 dcs.

Row 8: Ch 3, dc in next dc, * work 2 dcs in next ch-2 sp, [work 2 dcs in next dc, dc in next 3 dcs] twice; repeat from * across to last ch-2 sp, work 2 dcs in last ch-2 sp, dc in last 2 dcs, turn: 102 dcs.

Row 9: Ch 3, dc in next dc, ch 2, sk next 2 dcs, [dc in next 10 dcs, ch 2, sk 2 dcs] across to last 2 dcs, dc in last 2 dcs, turn: 9 ch-2 sps and 84 dcs.

Row 10: Ch 3, dc in next dc, * work 2 dcs in next ch-2 sp, [work 2 dcs in next dc, dc in next 4 dcs] twice; repeat from * across to last ch-2 sp, work 2 dcs in last ch-2 sp, dc in last 2 dcs, turn: 118 dcs.

Row 11: Ch 3, dc in next dc, ch 2, sk next 2 dcs, * [dc in next 5 dcs, work 2 dcs in next dc] twice, ch 2, sk 2 dcs; repeat from * across to last 2 dcs, dc in last 2 dcs, turn: 9 ch-2 sps and 116 dcs.

Row 12: Ch 3, dc in next dc, * work 2 dcs in next ch-2 sp, [dc in next 6 dcs, work 2 dcs in next dc] twice; repeat from * across to last ch-2 sp, work 2 dcs in last ch-2 sp, dc in last 2 dcs, turn: 150 dcs.

Row 13: Ch 3, dc in next dc, ch 2, sk next 2 dcs, * [dc in next 7 dcs, work 2 dcs in next st] twice, ch 2, sk 2 dcs; repeat from * across to last 2 dcs, dc in last 2 dcs, turn: 9 ch-2 sps and 148 dcs.

Row 14: Ch 3, dc in next dc, * work 2 dcs in next ch-2 sp, [dc in next 8 dcs, work 2 dcs in next dc] twice; repeat from * across to last ch-2 sp, work 2 dcs in last ch-2 sp, dc in last 2 dcs, turn: 182 dcs.

Row 15: Ch 3, dc in next dc, ch 2, sk next 2 dcs, * [dc in next 9 dcs, work 2 dcs in next st] twice, ch 2, sk 2 dcs; repeat from * across to last 2 dcs, dc in last 2 dcs, turn: 9 ch-2 sps and 180 dcs.

Row 16: Ch 3, dc in next dc, [work 2 dcs in next dc, dc in each dc to next ch-2 sp] across to last 4 dcs, work 2 dcs in last ch-2 sp, dc in last 2 dcs, turn: 198 dcs.

Row 17: Ch 3, dc in next dc, ch 2, sk next 2 dcs, * [dc in next 10 dcs, work 2 dcs in next st] twice, ch 2, sk 2 dcs;

repeat from * across to last 2 dcs, dc in last 2 dcs, turn: 9 ch-2 sps and 196 dcs.

Row 18: Ch 3, dc in next dc, * work 2 dcs in next ch-2 sp, [dc in next 11 dcs, work 2 dcs in next dc] twice; repeat from * across to last ch-2 sp, work 2 dcs in last ch-2 sp, dc in last 2 dcs, turn: 230 dcs.

Row 19: Ch 3, dc in next dc, ch 2, sk next 2 dcs, [dc in next 26 dcs, ch 2, sk next 2 dcs] across to last 2 dcs, dc in last 2 dcs, turn: 9 ch-2 sps and 212 dcs.

Row 20: Ch 3, dc in next dc, * work 2 dcs in next ch-2 sp, [dc in next 12 dcs, work 2 dcs in next dc] twice; repeat from * across to last ch-2 sp, work 2 dcs in last ch-2 sp, dc in last 2 dcs, turn: 246 dcs.

Row 21: Ch 3, dc in next dc, ch 2, sk next 2 dcs, [dc in next 28 dcs, ch 2, sk next 2 dcs] across to last 2 dcs, dc in last 2 dcs, turn: 9 ch-2 sps and 228 dcs.

Row 22: Ch 1, sl st in next dc, sl st in each of the chs of the ch-2 sp, sk next dc, * [work 5 dcs in next dc, sk next dc, sl st in next dc, sk next dc] seven times, sl st in each of the chs of the next ch-2 sp; repeat from * across to last 2 dcs, sl st in last 2 dcs. Fasten off.

Use yarn or tapestry needle to weave in all loose ends.

FINISHING: Ribbons with bows: Use quilter's marking pen and ruler to mark the coordinating red plaid fabric before cutting it with a scissors…or use rotary cutting tools to cut the fabric. Cut all strips crosswise from selvage to selvage.

Cut eight 1-1/2-in.-wide x 14-in.-long strips for ribbons.

Fold a strip in half lengthwise with right sides together. Sew long edges together with a narrow seam, leaving an opening for turning.

Center seam and sew across each narrow end with a narrow seam. Turn tube right side out. Turn raw edges in and hand-sew opening closed. Topstitch down center of ribbon if desired. Repeat to make a total of eight ribbons.

Cut eight 3-3/4-in. x 5-3/4-in. rectangles for bows. Fold a rectangle in half crosswise with right sides together to make a 3-3/4-in.-long rectangle.

Sew the long edges together with a narrow seam, leaving an opening for turning. Center seam and sew across each narrow end with a narrow seam. Turn piece right side out. Turn raw edges in and hand-sew opening closed. Repeat to make a total of eight rectangles for bows.

Referring to Fig. 1 above right, hand-sew across center of each rectangle and draw up thread to form bows. Fasten off.

With right side out, wrap one end of a ribbon around center of a bow, covering stitching. Hand-tack on back to hold ribbon in place. Sew one half of a snap to the wrong side of the opposite narrow

end of the ribbon.

Repeat to make a total of eight ribbons with bows.

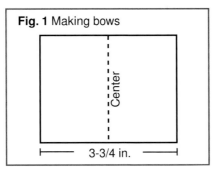

Fig. 1 Making bows

Center

3-3/4 in.

Tie: Cut one 3-in.-wide x 25-in.-long strip for center tie. Fold strip in half lengthwise with right sides together. Sew long edges together with a narrow seam, leaving an opening for turning. Center seam and sew across each narrow end with a narrow seam. Turn tie right side out. Turn raw edges in and hand-sew opening closed.

ASSEMBLY: Refer to photo on previous page as a guide while assembling the tree skirt as follows.

Place crocheted tree skirt right side up on a flat surface.

Overlap straight edges of the tree skirt and align eyelets along straight edges.

Starting at outer edge of the tree skirt and working toward the center, thread snap-end of a ribbon in and out of the overlapped eyelets.

Position the bow at the outer edge and pin to hold. Wrap snap-end of the ribbon to the inside of tree skirt. Sew other half of snap to the ribbon where needed to hold ribbon in place.

Add ribbons with bows to seven remaining rows of eyelets.

To put tree skirt around tree, remove ribbon from the overlapped eyelets. Wrap tree skirt right side out around base of tree and overlap straight edges as before.

Thread ribbon with bow through eyelets as before and snap to hold. Thread tie in and out of the 20 openings around the center of the tree skirt and tie ends in a bow. ☆

ABBREVIATIONS

ch(s)	chain(s)
dc(s)	double crochet(s)
hk	hook
sc(s)	single crochet(s)
sk	skip
sl st	slip stich
sp(s)	space(s)
tr(s)	treble(s)
* [ ]	Instructions following asterisk or between brackets are repeated as directed.

Seeds Sprout a Pretty Tree Trim

YOU MIGHT say Darlene Prazinak starts "scaring up" holiday craft projects as early as Halloween! That's when she collects the pumpkin seeds for these pretty poinsettias—a favorite for trimming her tree in Matlock, Manitoba or tying on gift packages.

Materials Needed:
About 26 clean dry pumpkin seeds
Whole mustard seeds
Red acrylic craft paint
Small flat paintbrush
1-1/2-inch circle of lightweight cardboard
1-3/4-inch circle of red felt
8-inch length of gold metallic thread for hanger
Clear glitter spray
Ruler
White (tacky) glue

Finished Size: Poinsettia measures about 2-3/4 inches across.

Directions:
Glue pumpkin seeds to the edge of the cardboard circle with the points facing outward and edges touching, making a circle that measures about 2-3/4 in. across.

Referring to the photo above for positioning of poinsettia leaves, glue remaining pumpkin seeds in second and third smaller circles with the points of each between the points of the previous layer. Let dry.

Paint the pumpkin seeds red. Let dry.

Glue whole mustard seeds in a mound in the center of the pumpkin seeds. Let dry.

Spray poinsettia with clear glitter spray following spray manufacturer's instructions. Let dry.

Glue ends of metallic thread to cardboard on back for hanging loop. Center and glue red felt circle to cardboard circle on back. Let dry.

Hang on your tree…or use to accent a gift package. ☆

Quilted Holder Pockets Season's Greetings

CHRISTMAS MEMORIES are often pieced together from cherished family traditions and keepsakes brought out every year just to make the season especially merry.

This cheery quilted card holder from Mary Cain of Sun Prairie, Wisconsin is destined to become one of those.

"I used a tree branch from my yard to accent the country look," Mary says, "and it warms up any wall I hang it on."

Materials Needed:

*44-inch-wide 100% cotton fabrics—
1/2 yard of beige print for front and backing; 1/4 yard of coordinating tree print for card pockets; 1/4 yard of muslin for lining card pockets; 1/8 yard each of white-on-white print, green dot and small green print for pieced checkerboard; and 1/8 yard of red print for border, sashing, binding and ties*

All-purpose thread to match fabrics

14-1/4-inch x 19-1/2-inch and 6-1/2-inch x 19-1/2-inch piece of lightweight quilt batting

Rotary cutter and mat (optional)

Quilter's marking pen or pencil

Quilter's ruler

Six 3/8-inch red buttons for trim on pieced checkerboard

One green and two red 3/4-inch buttons for trim on card pockets

Light brown and green six-strand embroidery floss or heavy thread

Embroidery needle
Standard sewing supplies
18-inch-long tree branch

Finished Size: Card holder is about 14-1/4 inches high x 19-1/2 inches wide without branch and hanging loops.

Directions:

CUTTING: Use quilter's marking pen and ruler to mark the fabrics before cutting them with a scissors, or use rotary cutting tools to cut the pieces as directed in instructions that follow. Cut strips crosswise from selvage to selvage.

From beige print, cut two 14-1/4-in. x 19-1/2-in. pieces for front background and backing of card holder.

From coordinating tree print, cut three 6-1/2-in. squares for card pockets.

From muslin, cut one 6-1/2-in. x 19-1/2-in. piece for lining card pockets.

From white-on-white print, cut three 1-1/2-in. x 13-in. strips for piecing checkerboard.

From green dot print, cut two 1-1/2-in. x 13-in. strips for piecing checkerboard.

From small green print, cut one 1-1/2-in. x 13-in. strip for piecing checkerboard.

From red print, cut two 1-in. x 6-1/2-in. strips for sashings between card pockets. For border of pieced checkerboard, cut two 1-in. x 15-1/2-in. strips and two 1-in. x 4-1/2-in. strips. Also cut one 2-1/4-in. x 19-1/2-in. strip for binding top of card pockets and two 2-1/4-in. x 44-in. strips for binding outer edge. For ties, cut two 2-in. x 20-in. strips.

PIECING: Do all stitching with right sides of fabrics together, edges even, matching thread and an accurate 1/4-in. seam allowance.

Card pockets: Referring to the photo for position and with the trees facing the same direction, lay out the three 6-1/2-in. squares of coordinating tree print and the two 1-in. x 6-1/2-in. red print sashing strips right side up between the squares. Sew the squares and sashing strips together as planned. Press the seams toward the sashing strips.

Place the 6-1/2-in. x 19-1/2-in. piece of muslin on a flat surface. Center the same-size piece of batting on top. With right side up, center pieced card pocket piece on top of batting. Pin layers together to hold.

With matching thread, sew an "X" through the center of each card pocket.

Thread embroidery needle with light brown floss or heavy thread. Sew a red button centered on the front of left-hand card pocket, leaving long tails on front of button. Tie tails in a knot on front of button and trim ends as desired. In the same way, sew a green button to the middle card pocket and a red button to the right-hand card pocket.

Fold the 2-1/4-in. x 19-1/2-in. red print binding strip in half lengthwise. With raw edges matching, sew binding to front of top edge of card pocket piece with a 1/4-in. seam. Fold binding to back, encasing raw edges.

With matching thread, stitch in-the-ditch of the seam, catching fold of binding on back.

Checkerboard: Sew a 1-1/2-in. x 13-in. white-on-white print strip to opposite long edges of a 1-1/2-in. x 13-in. green dot strip. Press seams toward darker fabric. Referring to Fig. 1a, cut eight 1-1/2-in. sections from pieced strip.

Sew a 1-1/2-in. x 13-in. green dot strip and a 1-1/2-in. x 13-in. small green print strip to opposite long edges of a 1-1/2-in. x 13-in. white-on-white print strip. Press seams toward darker fabrics. Referring to Fig. 1b, cut seven 1-1/2-in. sections from pieced strip.

Referring to photo, sew the long edges of the pieced sections together to

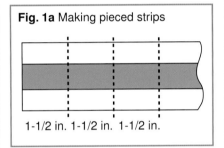

Fig. 1a Making pieced strips

1-1/2 in. 1-1/2 in. 1-1/2 in.

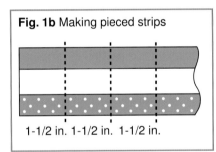

Fig. 1b Making pieced strips

1-1/2 in. 1-1/2 in. 1-1/2 in.

make a 3-1/2-in. x 15-1/2-in. pieced checkerboard.

Sew a 1-in. x 15-1/2-in. red print border strip to opposite long edges of pieced checkerboard. Open and press seams toward borders.

Sew a 1-in. x 4-1/2-in. red print border strip to opposite short edges of pieced checkerboard. Open and press seams toward borders.

Press 1/4 in. to wrong side on all edges of border.

ASSEMBLY: Refer to photo as a guide while assembling card holder as directed in the instructions that follow.

Place a 14-1/4-in. x 19-1/2-in. piece of background fabric for front of card holder right side up on a flat surface.

Place card pocket piece right side up on front piece, aligning side and bottom raw edges of pieces. Pin as needed to

hold in place.

Center pieced checkerboard right side up about 1-1/2 in. above the card pocket piece. Pin as needed to hold.

Place 14-1/4-in. x 19-1/2-in. piece of backing fabric wrong side up on a flat surface. Center 14-1/4-in. x 19-1/2-in. piece of batting on top of backing. Center assembled card holder front piece right side up on top of batting.

Sew around card holder, stitching 1/8 in. from outside edges.

With matching thread, stitch in-the-ditch of the seams of border around the pieced checkerboard and topstitch around the outer edge of the border.

Use embroidery needle and green floss or heavy thread to sew 3/8-in. red buttons to pieced checkerboard section of card holder.

With matching thread, topstitch down the center of each sashing strip between the card pockets, backstitching at the beginning and end of stitching.

BINDING: Sew short edges of binding strips together with a 1/4-in. seam. Press 1/4 in. to wrong side on one short edge of binding strip. Fold binding in half lengthwise with wrong sides together.

With raw edges matching, sew binding to front of card holder with a 1/4-in. seam, mitering corners.

Fold binding to back of card holder, encasing raw edges. With matching thread, stitch in-the-ditch of the binding seam, catching fold of binding on back.

TIES: Press each short end of a 2-in. x 20-in. red print strip 1/4 in. to the wrong side. Fold each long edge to the center of strip with wrong sides facing and press. Then fold strip in half lengthwise and press. Stitch down center of strip with matching thread. Repeat to make another tie.

Fold each tie in half crosswise to find the center. Referring to photo for position, pin center of each strip to the seam of top binding. With matching thread, stitch across center of each tie.

FINISHING: Place branch above top of card holder. Wrap each tie around branch and tie ends in a bow to form loops. ✫

Quilting Tips

● Several kinds of tape such as quilter's tape, masking tape, paper tape and painter's tape can be used as a guide for straight-line machine- or hand-quilting.

● Do not leave tape on your fabric for an extended period of time, as the adhesive may leave a residue on the fabric.

Fun Candy Cane Sweatshirt Sweetens Holiday for Kids

YOUNGSTERS will love sporting this merry candy cane motif for holiday gatherings or family get-togethers and photos.

Designed by Tammy LeBlanc from Geismar, Louisiana, the Christmasy red-and-white confection is quick and easy to complete. "The pattern could also be applied to an adult-size sweatshirt or canvas tote bag," Tammy suggests.

Materials Needed:

Pattern on next page
Tracing paper and pencil
Graphite paper
Stylus or dry ballpoint pen
White cotton/polyester blend
  sweatshirt
Foam plate or palette
Paper towels
Water container
Acrylic craft paints (Tammy used
  Apple Barrel)—Black, Cardinal
  Crimson, Cobalt Blue, Cranberry,
Country Gray, Hunter Green and
  White
Textile medium
Crystal glitter paint (Tammy used
  Polymark)
Paintbrushes—1/4-inch flat and
  1/2-inch flat
T-shirt board or heavy cardboard to fit
  inside sweatshirt
Waxed paper
Straight pins or clothespins
Masking tape

Finished Size: Painted design is about 4 inches wide x 7 inches high and is shown on a Child size Medium sweatshirt.

Directions:
Wash and dry sweatshirt following manufacturer's directions. Do not use detergents with built-in stain resistors or fabric softeners. Press if needed.

Trace pattern onto tracing paper with pencil.

Place a piece of waxed paper over

T-shirt board or cardboard to protect surface. With right side out, slip sweatshirt over T-shirt board or cardboard. Smooth front of sweatshirt and use pins or clothespins as needed to keep sweatshirt smooth without stretching it. Place sweatshirt on a flat surface.

Referring to photo for position, place pattern on front of sweatshirt and slip graphite paper between pattern and sweatshirt. Tape as needed to hold. Trace over lines of pattern with stylus or dry ballpoint pen to transfer pattern onto sweatshirt. Remove pattern and tape.

PAINTING: Place small amounts of each paint onto foam plate or palette as needed. Mix paints with textile medium prior to use, following textile medium manufacturer's instructions.

Refer to photo at left and pattern on next page as guides while painting as directed in the instructions that follow.

Use 1/2-in. flat brush and White to paint the white stripes on the candy cane.

Use 1/2-in. flat brush and Cardinal Crimson to paint the red stripes on the candy cane.

Use 1/4-in. flat brush and Country Gray to add shading to White stripes.

Use 1/4-in. flat brush and Cranberry to add shading to the Cardinal Crimson stripes.

Mix a small amount of White with Cardinal Crimson to make a lighter red. Use 1/4-in. flat brush and mixed paint to highlight the Cardinal Crimson stripes at the top of the candy cane.

Use 1/2-in. flat brush and Hunter Green to paint the holly leaves.

Mix a small amount of Black with Hunter Green to make a darker green. Use 1/4-in. flat brush and mixed paint to shade edges of holly leaves.

Mix two parts of White with one part Hunter Green to make a lighter green. Use 1/4-in. flat brush and mixed paint to highlight the tops of the holly leaves. With the chisel edge of the brush, add a center vein to each holly leaf.

Use 1/2-in. flat brush and Cobalt Blue to paint the bow and streamers.

Mix a small amount of Black with Cobalt Blue to make a darker blue. Use 1/4-in. flat brush and mixed paint to shade the edges of the bow and the bottoms of the streamers.

Mix a small amount of White with Cobalt Blue to make a lighter blue. Use 1/4-in. flat brush and mixed paint to highlight the top of the bow. With the chisel edge of the brush, add the details to the center of the bow.

After paint has dried completely, use 1/4-in. flat brush to generously apply glitter paint to top of the bow and streamers. Let dry.

Wrap as a special gift for a favorite youngster! ★

Handmade Paper Adds a Delicate Touch to Trim

THIS lovely paper ornament is as luminous as a snowflake with Christmas lights shining behind it.

Coni Gleason of Heber City, Utah designed the delicate three-dimensional trim that's a snap to make, light as air and can easily be folded flat to store. "I also tuck them into cards," she says.

Materials Needed:
Pattern below
Tracing paper and pencil
5-1/2-inch square of off-white construction paper or handmade paper (Coni used handmade mulberry paper)
Transparent tape
Craft knife or X-acto knife
Cutting mat
Round hole punch
8-inch length of six-strand blue embroidery floss
3/8-inch silver mushroom bead
Scissors

Finished Size: Paper ornament measures about 2-3/8 inches across.

Directions:
Trace pattern below onto tracing paper. Cut out pattern along outside lines.

Place traced pattern on center of piece of construction paper or handmade paper. Trace around outside of pattern onto paper. Then tape pattern as needed to hold it to the paper.

Using craft knife or X-acto knife, cut along inside dashed lines of traced pattern, cutting through pattern and paper and being careful not to cut past the center foldline of the pattern.

Use paper punch to make a hole in the top of the ornament where shown on pattern. Remove pattern.

Using scissors, cut out ornament, cutting just inside the pencil lines.

Thread one end of floss through punched hole in top of ornament. Slip 3/8-in. silver mushroom bead over both ends of floss. Tie ends of floss together to form a hanging loop. Position bead where desired. Tie floss in a knot to hold bead in place.

Referring to pattern, fold every other way along foldline to create a dimensional ornament. ✬

PAPER ORNAMENT PATTERN

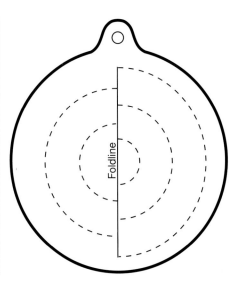

CHILD'S CANDY CANE SWEATSHIRT PATTERN
Trace 1—tracing paper
Paint as directed in instructions

73

Fun's Afoot with Gingerbread Stocking

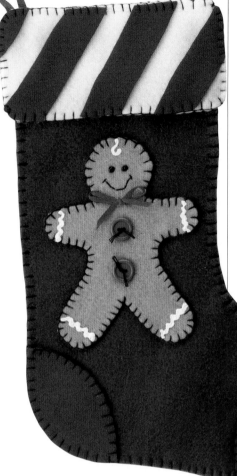

A STOCKING hung by the chimney with care is a sure sign of the magical promise of Christmas. This one, designed by Sheryl Radakovich of Portage, Indiana, sports a spunky gingerbread boy and candy-cane stripes.

"You don't even need a sewing machine—you simply blanket-stitch around the edge of the stocking with embroidery floss," Sheryl says. "And you can easily personalize it by adding a name with dimensional fabric paint."

Materials Needed:

Patterns on next page
Tracing paper and pencil
Felt—two 9-inch x 12-inch pieces of green for stocking; one 9-inch x 12-inch piece of white for cuff; 5-1/2-inch x 7-inch piece of red for stripes, heel and toe; and 4-1/2-inch x 6-inch piece of tan for gingerbread boy
Two 1/2-inch green two-hole buttons
Black six-strand embroidery floss
Embroidery needle
Black and white dimensional fabric/craft paints
6-inch length of 1/8-inch-wide red satin ribbon for bow
4-inch length of 1/4-inch-wide red satin ribbon for hanging loop
Straight pins
White (tacky) glue
Scissors

Finished Size: Gingerbread boy stocking is about 7-3/4 inches wide x 12 inches long without hanging loop.

Directions:

Use photocopier to enlarge patterns on next page to 200% and trace enlarged patterns onto tracing paper with pencil. Or draw a 1-in. grid on tracing paper and trace patterns as shown onto tracing paper with pencil.

Place the two pieces of green felt with wrong sides together and edges matching. Pin stocking pattern to felt. Cut out stocking, cutting through both layers of felt and pattern. Remove pattern.

Cut out four cuff pieces from white felt and one gingerbread boy from tan felt. Also cut out one heel and one toe piece from red felt.

Separate black six-strand embroidery floss and use two strands for backstitching and all blanket stitching. See Fig. 1 below right for stitch illustrations.

Backstitch mouth on gingerbread boy where shown on pattern.

Stitch around outside edge of gingerbread boy with a small blanket stitch.

Referring to pattern for placement, use three strands of black floss to sew buttons to front of gingerbread boy, leaving tails of floss on the front of each button. Knot floss on front of button. Trim floss ends as desired.

Tie the 1/8-in.-wide red satin ribbon in a small bow. Glue bow to neck of gingerbread boy. Let dry.

Use white dimensional paint to add wavy frosting lines where shown on gingerbread boy pattern. Let dry.

Use black dimensional paint to add two small dots to gingerbread boy for eyes. Let dry.

Referring to photo for placement, glue red felt stripes onto the front of one white felt cuff piece. Let dry.

Referring to pattern for placement, blanket-stitch around the inside edges of the red felt toe and heel pieces.

ASSEMBLY: Pin two green felt stocking pieces with wrong sides together and edges matching.

Referring to photo and pattern for placement, glue red felt toe and heel pieces to front of stocking with outside edges matching.

Stitch around stocking through both layers of felt with a large blanket stitch, leaving top straight edge unstitched.

Pin cuff piece with red stripes right side up to another white cuff piece with edges matching. Blanket-stitch along top and bottom edges, stitching through all layers.

Pin two remaining white cuff pieces together with edges matching, blanket-stitch along top and bottom edges, stitching through both layers of felt.

Fold 1/4-in.-wide red satin ribbon in half for hanging loop.

Layer the two joined cuff pieces with wrong sides together and edges matching. Slip ends of the hanging loop between the cuff pieces at the top left corner of the cuff.

Pin as needed to hold. Blanket-stitch side edges of the cuff together, stitching through all layers and making sure to catch the ends of the hanging loop in the stitching.

Referring to photo, slip cuff over the top of the stocking, lapping the stitched edge of the cuff over the top of the stocking as shown on the pattern.

Glue bottom overlapped portion of cuff to front and back of stocking. Let dry.

Referring to photo at left for position, glue gingerbread boy to front of stocking. Let dry.

Hang up stocking and wait for Santa to fill with goodies! ✫

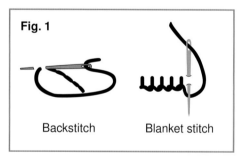

Fig. 1

Backstitch   Blanket stitch

KEY

——— Cutting/stitching line
– – – Overlapped portion of pattern

Bracelet Rounds Out Holiday Style with Bead-Dazzling Fun!

SPARKLY AND SHINY as a holiday night, this delicate wire-and-bead bracelet adds a festive twist to any Yuletide outfit.

Fashioned by Amy Burks of Midland, Michigan, the easy-to-craft jewelry makes a great last-minute gift or stocking stuffer for a favorite teacher or friend.

Or twirl it around napkins when setting your Christmas table (see page 110) for an elegant napkin ring that doubles as a keepsake party favor.

Materials Needed:
Bracelet-size stainless steel memory wire (found in craft stores with the jewelry findings)
Beads—34 size 2 green bugle beads; 51 size 10/0 red glass rocaille or seed beads; 30 clear E beads; 90 size 10/0 silver Indian seed beads; and 18 4mm silver beads
Needle-nose pliers
Wire cutters

Finished Size: Coiled beaded bracelet measures about 2-1/2 inches across and consists of two full coils and two three-quarter coils.

Directions:
Use needle-nose pliers to make a small loop at one end of the memory wire to hold beads on wire.

String beads onto the memory wire in the following order:

One 4mm silver bead, five silver Indian seed beads, * five clear E beads, [one green bugle bead, three red rocaille or seed beads, one green bugle bead, one 4mm silver bead and five silver Indian beads] three times; repeat from * until all beads have been added.

Slide beads down to end loop.

Use needle-nose pliers to make a small loop close to last bead added.

Use wire cutters to cut memory wire close to loop.

Catch the holiday's glow in your shimmery bracelet! ☆

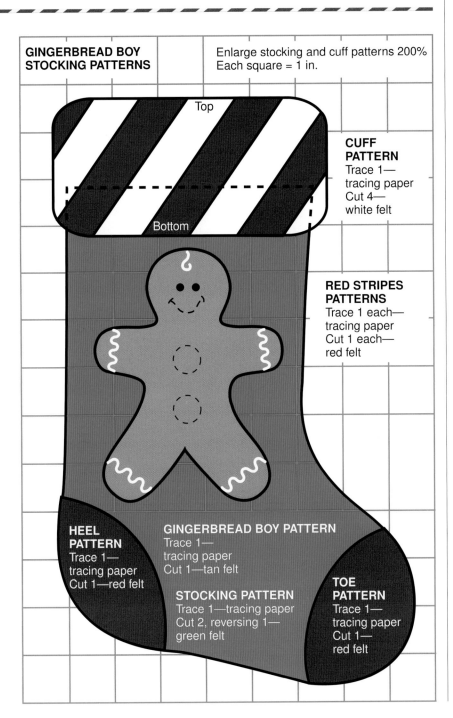

GINGERBREAD BOY STOCKING PATTERNS

Enlarge stocking and cuff patterns 200% Each square = 1 in.

Top

Bottom

CUFF PATTERN
Trace 1—tracing paper
Cut 4—white felt

RED STRIPES PATTERNS
Trace 1 each—tracing paper
Cut 1 each—red felt

HEEL PATTERN
Trace 1—tracing paper
Cut 1—red felt

GINGERBREAD BOY PATTERN
Trace 1—tracing paper
Cut 1—tan felt

STOCKING PATTERN
Trace 1—tracing paper
Cut 2, reversing 1—green felt

TOE PATTERN
Trace 1—tracing paper
Cut 1—red felt

BEADING KEY

[ ]   Instructions between brackets are repeated the number of times given.

*   Instructions following asterisk are repeated as directed.

75

Open the Door to Holiday-Style Welcome!

A BLIZZARD of blessings is what this little door hanger, designed by Kellie Montgomery of Lynn Haven, Florida, wishes all who cross its threshold.

In addition to brightening your own home decor for the holidays, the shiny bells on Frosty's tummy will jingle a wintry welcome to whomever enters. Add potpourri or lavender to the stuffing, and you have a quick gift for drop-in guests.

Materials Needed:

Patterns below
Tracing paper and pencil
Quilter's marking pen or pencil
Felt—two 6-1/2-inch x 9-1/2-inch pieces and two 1-inch x 12-inch pieces of medium blue and scraps each of white for snowman, red for scarf, black for hat and orange for nose
Three 6mm gold jingle bells
Two 1/2-inch red two-hole buttons
Six-strand embroidery floss—black, brown, dark blue, light blue, orange, red and white
Embroidery needle
Polyester stuffing
Straight pins
Pinking shears
Scissors

Finished Size: Door hanger measures about 9 inches across x 12 inches high.

Directions:

Trace patterns below onto tracing paper with pencil.

Cut out shapes from felt as directed on pattern.

Referring to photo at left and pattern for position, pin snowman, scarf, hat and nose to the right side of a 6-1/2-in. x 9-1/2-in. piece of medium blue felt, positioning the top and bottom of the snowman about 1/2 in. from the outside edge of the felt piece.

Separate six-strand floss and thread needle with three strands of floss for all stitching unless directions state otherwise. See Fig. 1 for stitch illustrations.

Using white, blanket-stitch around snowman.

Using black, blanket-stitch around hat.

Using red, stitch around the edges of the scarf where shown on the pattern

APPLIQUE KEY

— Outline/cutting line
- - - Overlapped portion of pattern
  x   Jingle bell placement
  ❧   French Knot
—— Backstich
- - - Running Stitch

BLESSINGS DOOR HANGER PATTERNS
Trace 1 each piece—tracing paper
Cut 1 each piece—color of felt indicated on pattern

Fig. 1

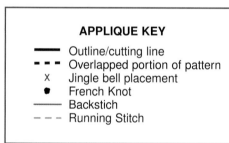

Backstitch

Blanket stitch

Running stitch

French knot

with a small running stitch.

Using red, backstitch the snowman's mouth and a small heart on the hat.

Using orange, stitch around the edges of the carrot nose with a running stitch.

Using dark blue, backstitch two lines across the hat for hat trim.

Using black, add two French knots for eyes.

Referring to photo for position, use six strands of brown to backstitch the two twig arms.

Referring to photo for position, use quilter's marking pen or pencil to write "Winter Blessings" freehand on left-hand side of front of felt piece.

Thread needle with three strands of white floss twisted with three strands of light blue floss and use combined floss to backstitch lettering. Add a French knot to dot each "i."

Use white floss to stitch snowflakes randomly around lettering and snowman. For each snowflake, stitch an X with a straight line across the center.

Use white floss to sew the jingle bells down the front of the snowman where shown on pattern.

Place remaining 6-1/2-in. x 9-1/2-in. medium blue felt piece on a flat surface. Place appliqued felt piece on top with right side up and edges matching. Pin as needed to hold.

Use black floss to sew a running stitch about 1/2 in. from all outside edges, stitching through both layers and stuffing the door hanger as you stitch around.

Use pinking shears to trim 1/4 in. from each outside edge of the door hanger.

Pin one end of each 1-in. x 12-in. medium blue felt strip to the back of opposite top corners.

Thread needle with two strands of white floss. On the front of the door hanger, sew a button to the top corners on each side, catching the felt strip on back in the stitching.

Tie ends of felt strips in square knot to form hanging loop.

Hang over a doorknob or picture hook and enjoy! ★

Craft Cute Clothespin Trims

TUCK these holly jolly trims on tree branches, perch them on candy cups for favors or use as stocking stuffers.

Crafter Loretta Mateik of Petaluma, California also uses them to add a festive flair to potted plants all through the house.

Materials Needed (for both):
Two 3/4-inch-long round slotted wooden clothespins
One 1-1/4-inch wooden doll head bead for snowman's head
1/2-inch length of 1/8-inch wooden dowel for snowman's nose
Purchased 1-5/8-inch-high x 3/16-inch-thick wooden gingerbread man
Drill with 1/8-inch bit
Finishing sandpaper
Paper towels
Foam plate or palette
Water container
Acrylic craft paints (Loretta used Delta Ceramcoat)—Black, Brown Iron Oxide, Chrome Green Light, Light Ivory, Mocha Brown, Moroccan Red, Pink Quartz and Tangerine
Paintbrushes—3/4-inch wash brush, 1/2-inch flat, small round and liner
Toothpick
Two 1/2-inch green pom-poms
2-1/4-inch length of 20-gauge gold craft wire for earmuffs
Two 1/2-inch rusty tin stars
White (tacky) glue

Finished Size: Snowman clothespin measures about 2-1/4 inches across x 4-3/4 inches high. Gingerbread clothespin measures about 1-3/8 inches across x 5-3/8 inches high.

Directions:
PAINTING: Keep paper towels and a container of water handy to clean brushes. Place dabs of each paint color on foam plate or palette as needed. Add coats of paint as needed for complete coverage.

Let paint dry after every application.

Refer to photo at right as a guide while painting as directed in the instructions that follow.

Gingerbread Clothespin: Use wash brush and Light Ivory to paint one entire clothespin.

Use wash brush and Mocha Brown to paint entire gingerbread shape.

Use flat brush and Brown Iron Oxide to shade around outside edges on one side (front) of gingerbread shape.

Use liner and Black to add two small dots for eyes and to add eyebrows and mouth to front of gingerbread shape.

Dip toothpick into Black and add three small dots for buttons.

Dip toothpick into Pink Quartz and add tiny dot for nose.

Use liner and Light Ivory to add a tiny dot in each eye.

Use round brush and Light Ivory to add hair and wavy lines of frosting to hands and feet.

Dip toothpick into Light Ivory and add tiny dots on both sides of each wavy frosting line.

Use flat brush and Moroccan Red to add diagonal stripes to clothespin.

Use liner and Chrome Green Light to add a thin line between the red stripes.

Use liner and Moroccan Red to add a thin line on both sides of each thin green line.

Glue gingerbread shape onto top of clothespin. Let dry.

Snowman Clothespin: Drill a 1/2-in.-deep hole into one side of doll head bead for snowman.

Use wash brush and Light Ivory to paint doll head bead and remaining clothespin.

Use sandpaper to round one end of wooden dowel piece for nose.

Use 1/2-in. brush and Tangerine to paint dowel piece for nose.

Glue flat end of nose into drilled hole in doll head bead. Glue head onto top of clothespin. Let dry.

Use liner and Black to add two tiny ovals for eyes and to add eyebrows.

Use liner and Light Ivory to add a tiny dot to each eye.

Dip flat brush into Moroccan Red. Wipe excess paint onto paper towel. With a nearly dry brush and circular motion, add cheeks to snowman's head.

Glue a pom-pom to each end of gold wire piece. Bend wire piece into an arc and glue pom-poms to opposite sides of snowman's head for earmuffs. Let dry.

Glue rusty tin stars down front of snowman. Let dry.

Make a clothesline full of these cute decorations! ★

Celebrate Those Baby Steps... With Holly-Trimmed Booties!

STITCH UP these adorable baby shoes as a sweet remembrance of Baby's first Christmas! The tiny plastic-canvas booties make a cherished family heirloom…and a cute tree ornament, too.

Susan Leinberger of Aiea, Hawaii designed the festive booties using sparkly metallic thread.

Materials Needed:

Charts on next page
One sheet of 10-count clear plastic canvas
Kreinik No. 32 Heavy Braid and Kreinik No. 12 Tapestry Braid in colors listed on color key
Size 18 tapestry needle
Patterns on page 79
Tracing paper and pencil
7-inch square of white adhesive-back felt for lining (Susan used Presto Felt by Kunin)
Two 3/8-inch silver jingle bells
Invisible (nylon) thread
Clear nail polish
Scissors

Finished Size: Each bootie is about 1-1/4 inches high x 2-1/4 inches long.

Directions:

CUTTING: Remembering to count the bars and not the holes, cut plastic canvas pieces as directed below.

Referring to charts on page 79, cut two 12-bar x 54-bar pieces for sides and two 12-bar x 22-bar pieces for year and lettering pieces of sole. Also cut two 8-bar x 12-bar pieces for tongue and two 5-bar x 8-bar pieces for toe of booties.

STITCHING: Cut 18-in. lengths of braid.

To keep the braid from raveling, dab a drop of clear nail polish onto the ends of each piece and let polish dry before stitching.

Do not knot braid on back of work. Instead, leave a 1-in. tail of braid on back of the plastic canvas and work the next few stitches over it. To end, run braid on back of canvas under completed stitches of the same color and clip close to work. See Fig. 1 on the next page for stitch illustrations.

Make two of each piece as directed in the instructions that follow.

Sole: Using Pearl Heavy Braid and following the sole charts, stitch each sole piece with Continental stitches, leaving outside edges unstitched.

Using Crimson Tapestry Braid and following the lettering chart, backstitch "baby's 1st Christmas" on the right side of one sole piece.

Using Crimson Tapestry Braid and following the number chart, backstitch the year on the right side of remaining sole piece.

Side: Using Pearl Heavy Braid and following the chart, stitch side piece with Continental and reverse Continental stitches, leaving outside edges unstitched.

Using Emerald Heavy Braid and straight stitches, stitch holly on side piece.

Using Crimson Heavy Braid, add French knots where shown on chart.

Using Silver Heavy Braid, overcast top edge of each side piece.

Tongue and toe: Using Pearl Heavy Braid, stitch each tongue piece and each toe piece with Continental stitches, leaving outside edges unstitched.

Using Silver Heavy Braid, overcast long edges and one short edge of each tongue piece.

Lining: Trace a sole lining and side lining patterns onto tracing paper with pencil.

Cut two sole pieces and two side pieces from white felt.

Remove paper backing and adhere felt pieces centered on wrong side of matching stitched pieces.

Assembly: Use Pearl Heavy Braid for all whipstitching.

With right sides out, whipstitch the bottom edge of one side piece to the outside edge of one sole piece, starting and stopping stitching where shown on sole charts. Repeat with remaining side and sole pieces.

With right sides out, whipstitch toe piece to side piece, beginning along the short side of the side piece and continuing along the front of the sole to the end of the other side of the toe piece.

With right sides out, whipstitch the remaining edge of the toe piece to one short edge of the tongue piece.

Repeat to assemble other bootie.

FINISHING: Thread needle with invisible thread and tack opposite upper edge of each tongue to opposite top edges of each bootie.

Lacing: Thread needle with a 12-in. length of Emerald Heavy Braid.

Working from the bottom to the top and centering jingle bell on top of toe, insert needle from the inside to the outside on each side of bootie where shown on side chart. Knot braid at the top of the bootie and then tie a small bow. Secure bow with a drop of clear nail polish. Let dry.

Repeat to lace up other bootie.

Hanging loop: Thread needle with a 10-in. length of Emerald Heavy Braid. Attach each end of braid to center back of each bootie where shown on chart.

Tie a small bow in top of hanging loop. Secure bow with a drop of clear nail polish. Let dry.

Tie to Baby's first tree! ★

BABY'S 1ST CHRISTMAS ORNAMENT CHARTS

SIDE CHART
12 bars x 54 bars
Cut 2—plastic canvas

TOE CHART
5 bars x 8 bars
Cut 2—plastic canvas

TONGUE CHART
8 bars x 12 bars
Cut 2—plastic canvas

SOLE CHART (YEAR)
12 bars x 22 bars
Cut 1—plastic canvas

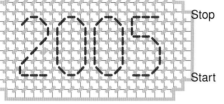
Stop
Start

SOLE CHART (LETTERING)
12 bars x 22 bars
Cut 1—plastic canvas

Stop
Start

NUMBER CHART

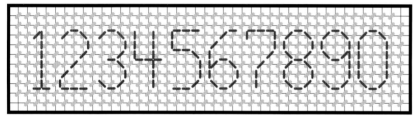

COLOR AND STITCH KEY
CONTINENTAL STITCH
Pearl Heavy Braid
REVERSE CONTINENTAL STITCH
Pearl Heavy Braid
BACKSTITCH
Crimson Tapestry Braid
STRAIGHT STITCH
Emerald Heavy Braid
OVERCAST/WHIPSTITCH
Pearl Heavy Braid
Silver Heavy Braid
FRENCH KNOT
Crimson Heavy Braid
Crimson Tapestry Braid

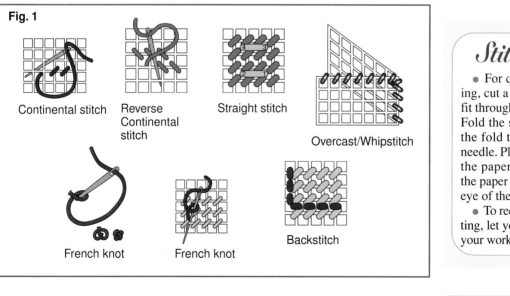

Fig. 1

Continental stitch
Reverse Continental stitch
Straight stitch
Overcast/Whipstitch
French knot
French knot
Backstitch

Stitching Tips

● For quick-and-easy threading, cut a strip of paper that will fit through the eye of the needle. Fold the strip in half and insert the fold through the eye of the needle. Place the thread between the paper ends and gently pull the paper and thread through the eye of the needle.

● To reduce tangling and knotting, let your needle dangle from your work after a few stitches.

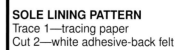

SIDE LINING PATTERN
Trace 1—tracing paper
Cut 2—white adhesive-back felt

SOLE LINING PATTERN
Trace 1—tracing paper
Cut 2—white adhesive-back felt

Tree Trim Makes Spirits Bright With True Meaning of Christmas

ROCK-A-BYE BABY Jesus in your Christmas treetop…Linda McConoughey of Rockford, Illinois designed this sweet swaddled reminder of the reason for the season.

Follow her instructions and craft a baby, basket and star for a treasured trim you'll look forward to hanging on your tree year after year.

Materials Needed:

No. 0 or No. 1 round natural reed
Heavy scissors or side cutters
Ruler or tape measure
Large plastic bucket to soak reed
Old towel
Large rubber band
Screwdriver or awl
2-inch-high x 1/8-inch-thick wooden star
1-3/16-inch-long wooden doll body for baby
Drill with 1/8-inch bit
Finishing sandpaper
Tack cloth
Foam plate or palette
Paper towels
Water container
Acrylic craft paints—brown, flesh, light gold, medium gold and dark gold
Small flat paintbrush
Matte spray sealer
Black fine-line marker
Natural excelsior
4-inch square of unbleached muslin
Small amount of polyester stuffing
3-1/2-inch length of 24-gauge gold craft wire for halo
16-inch length of natural hemp string for hanging loop
Glue gun and glue stick
Scissors

Finished Size: Ornament measures about 3 inches across x 8 inches high.

Directions:

Referring to photo above right for position, drill a hole through four points of the star.

Sand wood pieces smooth and wipe each clean with tack cloth.

WEAVING: Soak reed in warm water until pliable before using.

Use screwdriver or awl to pack the rounds tightly together.

Basket bottom: For spokes, cut two 20-in.-long pieces of reed. On wrong side, mark center of each spoke.

Place towel on a flat surface.

Referring to Fig. 1 below left, place spokes on towel in an X shape.

Cut a 13-in.-long piece of reed for fifth spoke. Referring to Fig. 2 below, add fifth spoke by weaving reed piece around the spokes in an over one, under one pattern as shown and turning the end outward on the final round for use as the fifth spoke.

Weave around with another long piece of natural reed in an over one, under one pattern, pushing the reed close together and spacing the spokes evenly apart after a couple of rounds.

Continue weaving to make an oval for the basket bottom that measures about 2 in. wide x 2-1/2 in. long.

Basket sides: Carefully bend the spokes up and hold them in place with the large rubber band.

Weave around in an over one, under one pattern until the basket is about 3/4 in. high.

Tuck end of reed to inside of basket and trim excess.

Twining rim: Bend spokes to inside of basket and weave the ends back through the sides and into the inside of the bottom of the basket. Clip excess reed.

Referring to Fig. 3 below right, use another reed to twine around the three top reeds for three rounds. Tuck end to inside of basket and trim excess.

Finishing: Thin brown paint with clean water to an ink-like consistency. Use flat brush to apply thinned paint to entire basket. Let dry.

PAINTING: Keep paper towels and

a container of water handy to clean brushes. Place dabs of each paint color onto foam plate or palette as needed. Paint all sides of wood pieces as directed. Add coats of paint as needed for complete coverage. Let paint dry after every application.

Use flat brush and flesh to paint entire doll body for baby.

Use flat brush and medium gold to paint entire star.

Dip flat brush into light gold and wipe excess paint off onto paper towel. With a nearly dry brush and a circular motion, highlight the center of one side of star.

In the same way, use flat brush and dark gold to shade the outside edges of the same side of the star.

Spray wood pieces with sealer, following manufacturer's instructions. Let dry.

FINISHING: Use the black marker to

Fig. 1 Laying out spokes

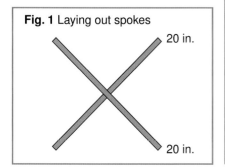

20 in.

20 in.

Fig. 2 Adding fifth spoke

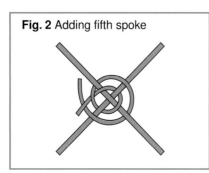

Fig. 3 Twining top

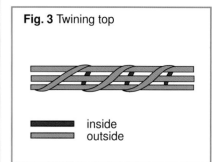

inside
outside

write "Wise men still seek Him!" on front of star.

Fill inside of basket with natural excelsior and glue as needed to hold.

Following grain of fabric, trim 1/4 in. from each side of muslin square, leaving a 3-1/2-in. square. Pull threads from all sides of muslin square to fringe.

Place baby diagonally on muslin square. Place a bit of stuffing around the baby and wrap muslin around for blanket. Glue blanket as needed to hold.

Form gold wire piece into a 3/4-in. cir-cle for halo and twist ends together to hold. Glue ends of wire under baby's head, leaving circle of wire exposed for halo.

Glue wrapped baby to top of excelsior in basket.

Cut a 6-in. length of hemp string. Thread ends of string from the back to the front through two opposite holes in top of star. Tie ends in a knot on the front of the star for hanging loop. Trim excess string close to knot.

Cut two 5-in. lengths of hemp string.

Tie one end of each length of hemp string to opposite sides of the top of the basket. Thread the other end of the left-hand string from the back to the front of the hole in the bottom left-hand point of the star. Knot the end on the front of the star.

In the same way, attach the remaining length of string to the right-hand point of the star. Adjust knots as needed so basket hangs straight and level. Trim ends of string close to knots.

Use this starry delight to brighten up holiday boughs! ✫

Ruffle Trim Fills Bushels of Yuletide Uses!

A-TISKET, A-TASKET…here's a simple but versatile way to dress up holiday baskets!

Crafter Jean Devore of Jackson, Missouri says, "These ruffles are fun, really easy to make and can be used in so many ways during the holidays.

"The large basket ruffle makes a great table topper, but you could also make smaller ruffles to slip over gift tins of cookies and fudge or to dress up soap baskets in guest baths."

Materials Needed:
12-inch-wide x 18-inch-long x 6-inch-high basket or other size basket of your choice
1 yard of 44-inch-wide 100% cotton or cotton-blend Christmas print fabric*
Matching all-purpose thread
1/2-inch-wide elastic—amount equal to distance around sides of basket minus 2 inches
2 yards of ribbon of choice (Jean used a 3-inch-wide gold metallic ribbon)
Safety pin
Standard sewing supplies

* The amount of fabric needed will vary depending on the size of your basket. See directions below for determining yardage for other size baskets.

Finished Size: Basket ruffle is 5-1/2 inches wide and is shown on a 12-inch-wide x 18-inch-long x 6-inch-high basket.

Directions:
Measure the height of the sides of your basket. Double that measurement and subtract 2 in. This will be the width of the fabric.

Measure the distance around your basket and multiply that number by 2 for the length of the fabric. See Fig. 1.

Cut the number of crosswise strips of fabric as needed to achieve the desired

length and the determined width measurement. (It is not necessary to trim the strips to the precise length. Extra length gives extra fullness.)

With right sides together and a 1/2-in. seam, sew the short ends of the strips together to make one long strip. Press seams open.

With the right sides together, sew the remaining short ends together, leaving a 3/4-in.-long opening 1 in. from one long edge for inserting the elastic. Press seam open.

Fold tube in half with wrong sides together and long raw edges matching.

With right side up, sew long raw edges together with a medium satin stitch.

Using a straight stitch, sew a 3/4-in.-wide casing about 1 in. from satin-stitched edge for elastic.

Attach safety pin to one end of elastic. Thread elastic through the casing, being careful not to twist the elastic.

Stitch ends of elastic together.

Distribute fabric evenly along elastic. Slip ruffle right side out over basket.

Form ribbon into a large multi-loop bow with streamers.

Hand-tack bow to ruffle where desired.

Fill your Christmas basket with gift packages, sewing notions, pretty soaps or pinecones and greenery. ✫

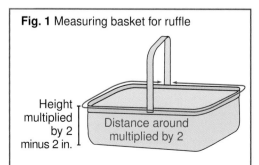

Fig. 1 Measuring basket for ruffle

Height multiplied by 2 minus 2 in.

Distance around multiplied by 2

Bolster Your Holiday Decor with Pretty Pillow

ACCENT your family room or couch with a colorful splash of Christmas spirit! Here's a cozy knit pillow that wishes "Happy Holly Days" to all those Yuletide visitors who come to call.

Brigitte Cornell of Copperas Cove, Texas designed the cute cushion and trimmed it with cheery red buttons. "This pillow is a snap for intermediate crafters and makes a warm and wonderful gift idea," Brigitte notes.

Materials Needed:
Chart on next page
4-ply worsted-weight acrylic yarn (Brigitte used Red Heart Super Saver yarn)—one 3.5-ounce skein of White and scraps each of Hot Red, Honey Gold and Paddy Green
Size 8 (5mm) straight knitting needles or size needed to obtain correct gauge
15-1/2-inch x 16-inch piece of coordinating Christmas print fabric for back of pillow
Four 1/2-inch two-hole red buttons
14-inch square pillow form
Size 16 tapestry needle
Scissors

Gauge: When working in St st on size 8 needles, 16 sts and 22 rows = 4 inches. To save time, take time to check gauge.

Stitches Used:
STOCKINETTE STITCH: St st:
   Row 1 (RS): K across row.
   Row 2 (WS): P across row.
   Repeat Rows 1 and 2 as directed.

Finished Size: Pillow is about 15 inches square.

Directions:
Holly and letters are made by duplicate st after background is knit. Refer to chart on next page for pattern.
   BACKGROUND: With size 8 needles and White yarn, cast on 61 sts.
   Row 1: * K 1, p 1; repeat from * across to last st, k 1.
   Rows 2-5: Repeat Row 1.
   Row 6: (RS): K 1, p 1, k 1, p 1, k across to last 4 sts, p 1, k 1, p 1, k 1.
   Row 7 (WS): K 1, p 1, k 1, p 1, k 1, p across to last 5 sts, k 1, p 1, k 1, p 1, k 1.
   Rows 8-83: Repeat Rows 6 and 7.
   Rows 84-88: Repeat Rows 1-5.
   DUPLICATE STITCHING: Each square on the chart equals one V-shaped duplicate stitch. See Fig. 1 for stitch illustration.

Thread tapestry needle with a single strand of yarn. Do not knot yarn. To begin stitching, leave a short tail of yarn on back of work and hold in place while working the first few stitches around it. To end stitching, weave yarn through stitches on back of work before cutting.

Follow the color key and chart on next page to stitch design on the right side of the knit piece.

FINISHING: Place knit piece and fabric for backing of pillow with right sides together and top and side edges matching. Turn bottom edge of fabric to wrong side for hem. Fold of hem should be even with bottom edge of border of knit front.

Thread tapestry needle with White yarn. Backstitch edges of knitted border to edge of backing fabric with a 1/4-in. seam, leaving bottom edge open. See Fig. 2 for stitch illustration.

Turn pillow right side out and insert pillow form.

Use tapestry needle and White yarn to sew buttons evenly spaced along inside of hem.

Slip buttons through the knit border on the front to close.

Toss pillow where needed for a touch of holly-day hues! ★

ABBREVIATIONS	
k	knit
p	purl
RS	right side
St(s)	stitch(es)
WS	wrong side
*	Instructions following asterisk are repeated as directed.

KNIT PILLOW CHART

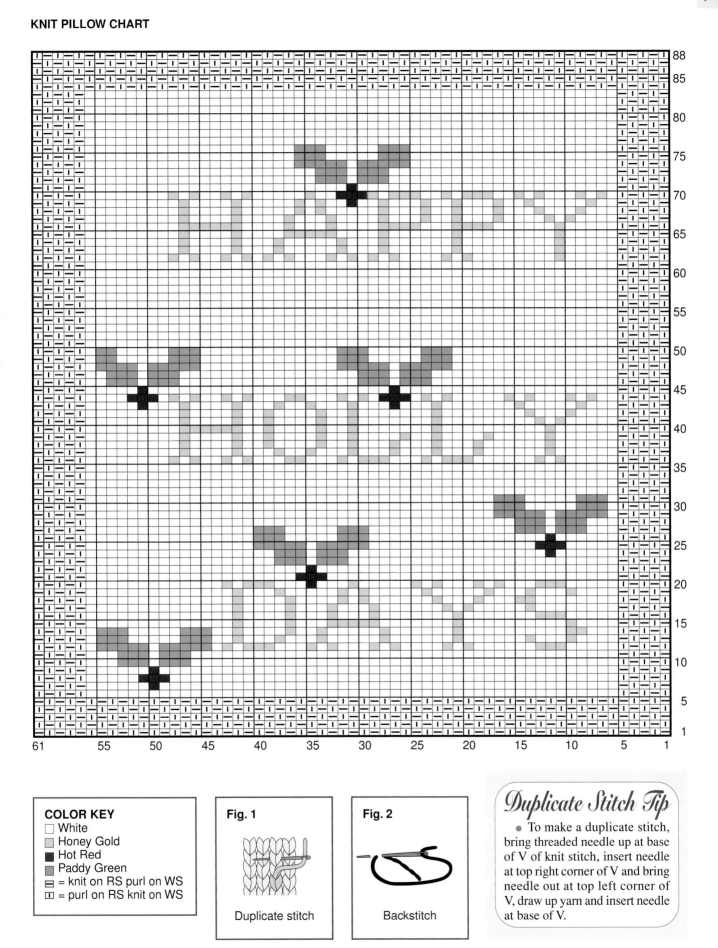

COLOR KEY
- ☐ White
- Honey Gold
- Hot Red
- Paddy Green
- ⊟ = knit on RS purl on WS
- ⊡ = purl on RS knit on WS

Fig. 1

Duplicate stitch

Fig. 2

Backstitch

Duplicate Stitch Tip

- To make a duplicate stitch, bring threaded needle up at base of V of knit stitch, insert needle at top right corner of V and bring needle out at top left corner of V, draw up yarn and insert needle at base of V.

Weave Some Christmas Magic With Old-Time Basket Trim

WHAT A TREASURE this tiny hand-woven basket will make hanging from a country Christmas tree or tied to a holiday gift!

Follow the easy instructions of Emmaus, Pennsylvania crafter Elizabeth Cramsey to create the distinctive rustic ornament that's sure to be cherished for years to come.

Materials Needed:

Natural reed—3/8-inch flat for stakes and 1/4-inch flat for weavers
Green reed*—3/16-inch flat oval or 1/4-inch flat for trim
3-inch x 4-inch D handle
Heavy scissors or side cutters
Ruler and pencil
Large plastic bucket to soak reed
Old towel
Large rubber band
Screwdriver or awl
5/8-inch two-hole natural wood button
6-inch length of 3-ply green jute string or heavy green thread
Paper towels
Foam plate or palette
Water container
Acrylic craft paints—dark red and light brown
Small flat paintbrush
3/4-inch x 4-inch torn fabric strip
Scissors

*To dye your own reed, use green basket dye or Rit dye and follow the dye manufacturer's instructions.

Finished Size: Basket ornament is about 3-1/4 inches long x 1-1/4 inches wide x 4 inches high.

Directions:

PAINTING: Keep paper towels and container of water handy to clean brushes. Place dabs of each paint color on foam plate or palette as needed. Add coats of paint as needed for complete coverage. Let paint dry after every application.

Paint button dark red. Let dry.

Cut a 2-in. length of 1/4-in. reed for tree trunk. Paint tree trunk light brown. Let dry.

WEAVING: Basket: Before using, soak reed in warm water for about 5 minutes or until pliable.

Tuck ends of weavers under stake or handle at end of row and trim so weaver does not show.

Use screwdriver or awl to pack the rows tightly together.

For stakes, cut three 10-in.-long pieces of 3/8-in. natural reed. On wrong side, mark center of each stake.

Measure and mark the centers on wrong side of stakes.

Place towel on a flat surface. Stand D handle upright on top of towel.

Referring to Fig. 1 at right, place first 3/8-in. stake under handle, the second over the handle and the third under the handle, leaving about 1/2 in. between stakes.

Carefully bend all stakes up along both long sides of handle to form bottom of basket.

Place rubber band around stakes to hold them upright.

Row 1: Starting on the outside of the first stake on the left, weave around with 1/4-in. natural reed in an over one, under one pattern.

Row 2: Weave around, starting on the outside of the center stake and alternating over and under the stakes.

Rows 3-10: Repeat Rows 1 and 2.

Rim: Bend stakes to inside of basket and tuck the ends under the first three rows of weaving.

Tree: Cut a 16-in. length of green reed.

With rough side facing out, tuck one end of green reed piece under the right-hand side of middle stake in the second row from the top. Wrap reed to the left and thread end from the left to the right under middle stake in the fourth row from the top, leaving a loop of reed on the front.

Wrap reed to the left and thread end from the left to the right under middle stake in the sixth row from the top, leaving a larger loop of reed on the front. In the same way, thread reed through eighth reed from the top and leave a larger loop. To end, tuck end of green reed between the reed in the eighth row and the right side of the handle.

Trunk: Insert one end of light brown reed piece between middle stake on the front and the top of the handle. Tuck other end of piece under reed in fourth row from the bottom of the basket.

FINISHING: Insert end of jute string or heavy green thread under middle stake of top row on front of basket. Thread ends from back to front through holes in button. Tie ends in an overhand knot on the front of the button. Trim ends as desired.

Wrap fabric strip around handle and tie ends in an overhand knot. Trim ends as desired. Tuck a small gift or gold candy coins inside! ✩

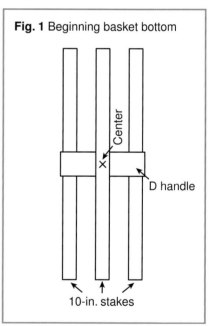

Fig. 1 Beginning basket bottom

Center

×

D handle

10-in. stakes

Basket Ornament Tips

• Be sure to wipe colored reed to remove excess moisture so color does not bleed onto natural reed.

• If you plan to make several of the same basket, cut all the stakes at once. Twist-tie the stakes together in one bundle for each basket.

Recycled Bulbs Make Bright Gift Ideas

BETTER WATCH OUT...for burned-out lightbulbs and night lights, that is! You can easily craft them into fun and thrifty gifts, thanks to clever designer Susan Newberry of DeFuniak Springs, Florida. She turns the burned-out bulbs into eye-catching Santa trims and tiny pins.

"These make a fun and easy family project—or cute gifts for teachers," she says. "Kids like slipping the fingers of knit gloves onto the tiny bulbs for hats."

So gather the family round, put on some carols and craft up a crowd of Kris Kringles—in all sizes!

Materials Needed (for both):
Foam plate or palette
Paper towels
Water container
Acrylic craft paints—black, flesh, red and white
Paintbrushes—small flat and small round
Toothpick
Textured snow medium
Wooden craft stick
Glue gun and glue sticks
Scissors

Materials Needed (for ornament):
Standard lightbulb
1/4-inch natural wooden bead for nose

8-inch x 10-inch piece of red solid flannel or cotton fabric for hat
1/2-inch-wide x 8-inch-long strip of white fur fabric for trim on hat
1/2-inch gold jingle bell
Artificial holly for trim on hat
Small amount of polyester stuffing
24-inch length of gold craft wire
Ruler
Tracing paper and pencil
Straight pins

Materials Needed (for pin):
Night-light bulb
1/8-inch natural wooden bead for nose
Knit finger cut from red solid knit glove
1/2-inch white pom-pom
1-inch pin back

Finished Size: Santa ornament measures about 2-1/2 inches across x 4-1/2 inches high without hanging loop. Santa pin measures about 1 inch across x 3 inches high.

Directions:
SANTA ORNAMENT: Using flat brush, paint entire standard-size lightbulb white. Let dry.

Refer to photo at left as a guide while painting and assembling ornament as directed in the instructions that follow.

Use flat brush and flesh to paint an oval on one side of lightbulb for Santa's face and to paint the wooden bead for his nose. Let dry.

Dip flat brush into red and wipe excess paint onto paper towel. With a nearly dry brush and a circular motion, add cheeks to Santa's face. Let dry.

Use round brush and black to add two eyes. Let dry.

Dip toothpick into white and add two small dots to each eye and a tiny dot to each cheek. Let dry.

Glue wooden bead below eyes for nose. Let dry.

Use wooden craft stick to apply a thick coat of textured snow medium to the rest of the lightbulb and to add eyebrows. Let dry.

Glue polyester stuffing around base of lightbulb. Let dry.

Referring to Fig. 1, draw hat pattern onto tracing paper. Pin pattern to right side of red solid fabric. Cut out hat.

Wrap longest edge of hat around base of lightbulb, overlapping excess fabric in back. Glue overlapped fabric for seam in back. Glue hat to lightbulb as needed to hold.

Wrap fur fabric trim around bottom edge of hat, overlapping ends in back. Trim excess.

Glue tip of hat to left side of hat and jingle bell to tip of hat. Let dry.

Glue holly trim to right side of hat. Let dry.

Thread end of craft wire through top of hat. With ends even, twist wire to form a hanging loop. Wrap ends of wire around pencil to coil. Remove pencil.

SANTA PIN: Using flat brush, paint entire night-light bulb white. Let dry.

Refer to photo below as a guide while painting and assembling pin as directed in the instructions that follow.

Use flat brush and flesh to paint an oval on one side of light-bulb for Santa's face and to paint the wooden bead for his nose. Let dry.

Dip flat brush into red and wipe excess paint onto paper towel. With a nearly dry brush and a circular motion, add cheeks to Santa's face.

Use round brush and black to add two eyes. Let dry.

Dip toothpick into white. Add tiny dot to each eye. Let dry.

Glue the wooden bead below eyes for nose. Let dry.

Use wooden craft stick to apply a thick coat of textured snow medium to rest of lightbulb and to add eyebrows. Let dry.

Fold open end of knit finger from glove up to form cuff of hat. Slip hat over top of bulb and glue to hold. Glue pom-pom to top of hat. Let dry.

Use craft stick to apply a bit of textured snow to top of hat. Let dry.

Glue pin back to back of Santa's hat. Let dry. ✫

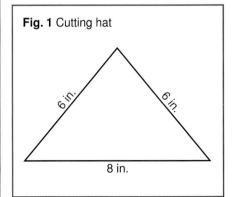

Fig. 1 Cutting hat

6 in.   6 in.

8 in.

Snowman Celebrates Winter with Hearty Joy!

JAUNTY and jolly, here's a snowman that's certain to melt hearts and bring warm smiles to family, friends and Christmas visitors.

Follow Corning, New York crafter Irene Wegener's simple directions to create your own festive version. "Start to finish, you can put this fellow together in just about an hour," she says.

Materials Needed:
Pattern on next page
Tracing paper and pencil
5-inch square of dark red solid flannel for appliqued heart
Cotton quilt batting—8-inch x 16-inch piece for head, 11-inch x 20-inch piece for middle body section and 14-inch x 26-1/2-inch piece for bottom body section
11-inch x 17-inch piece of dark red Polarfleece for hat

5-inch x 33-inch torn strip of coordinating plaid fabric for scarf
4 cups of plastic doll pellets or uncooked rice
Polyester stuffing
Two 8mm black seed beads for eyes
1-1/2-inch length of 1/4-inch wooden dowel for nose
Craft knife
Orange acrylic craft paint
Small flat paintbrush
Heavy black thread or pearl cotton
Embroidery needle
Powdered cosmetic blush
Buttons—one 7/8-inch dark blue, one 1-inch dark red and one 1-1/4-inch dark blue
Two 1-1/2-inch white plastic snowflakes
Two 6-inch-long forked twigs for arms
Glue gun and glue sticks
Hairspray
Crystal glitter
Standard sewing supplies

Finished Size: Snowman measures about 16 inches across x 20 inches tall.

Directions:
Use craft knife to trim one end of 1-1/2-in. length of wooden dowel to a point for nose.

Paint nose orange. Let dry.

Trace heart pattern on next page onto tracing paper with pencil as directed on pattern.

Cut out heart from dark red flannel.

Fold each piece of cotton quilt batting in half crosswise with the right sides together.

With matching thread, sew short edges of each together with a narrow seam to make tubes. Turn each tube right side out.

Thread hand-sewing needle with double strand of white thread. Sew around one raw edge of each tube with a running stitch 1/4 in. from one raw edge. See Fig. 1 below for stitch illustration. Pull thread to close one end of each tube, fastening off each.

Sew a running stitch around opposite raw edge of largest tube, leaving thread attached. Pour plastic doll pellets or uncooked rice into tube. Stuff tube firmly with stuffing. Draw up thread to close and fasten off.

In same way, sew a running stitch around the raw edge of each remaining tube. Stuff each tube firmly with stuffing. Pull thread to close each opening and fasten off each.

Place the bottom (largest) section of snowman on a flat surface with the stuffing-end up. With seams aligned up the back, glue a gathered edge of the center middle body section to the gathered top of the bottom body section. In the same way, glue head to the gathered top of middle body section. Let dry.

Referring to photo above left for position, pin heart right side up to front of bottom body section.

Thread embroidery needle with black heavy thread or pearl cotton and sew heart to snowman with long straight stitches. Add mouth to front of head with long running stitches. See Fig. 1 below for

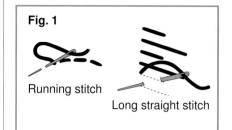
Fig. 1
Running stitch
Long straight stitch

86

stitch illustrations.

Hand-sew buttons to front of middle body section.

Use paintbrush and circular motion to apply powdered blush to cheeks.

Use scissors to cut a small hole in center of head for nose. Glue flat end of nose into opening. Let dry.

Use black heavy thread or pearl cotton to sew beads to head just above nose for eyes.

Fold fabric for hat in half crosswise with right sides together. Sew short edges together with narrow seam to make a tube. Turn tube right side out. Fold 1-1/2 in. twice to the outside for cuff of hat.

Place hat on snowman's head with seam in back. Hand-gather open end together. Tie piece of heavy black thread or pearl cotton around top of hat 3 in. from open edge. Spot-glue hat to head as needed to hold. Let dry.

Use scissors to cut small slits on opposite sides of middle body section of snowman for arms. Glue ends of forked twigs into openings. Let dry.

Wrap scarf around snowman's neck and tie ends in a loose overhand knot.

Glue a snowflake to knot of scarf and top of hat. Let dry.

Spray entire snowman with hairspray. While hairspray is still wet, sprinkle snowman with crystal glitter. Let dry. Tap off the excess glitter.

Set this frosty fellow out where he can tickle the fancy of holiday guests!

SNOWMAN PATTERN

HEART PATTERN
Trace 1—tracing paper
Cut 1—dark red flannel

Trace, flop and repeat for complete pattern

Grain

Necklace Is Alight With Colors Bright

CRAFTER Helen Rafson of Louisville, Kentucky came up with this bright idea for lighting up the Christmas season!

Using beads and blanket-stitched felt tree lights, she fashioned the festive accent for sweatshirts, sweaters and more casual clothes. "It also makes a quick stocking stuffer for girls of all ages," Helen adds.

Materials Needed:
Patterns below right
Tracing paper and pencil
Felt—two 2-inch squares each of turquoise, green, purple, orange, yellow and red and one 3-inch square of gold
Black six-strand embroidery floss
Embroidery needle
Polyester stuffing
24-inch length of 1/8-inch black satin cording
11 gold pony beads
Jewelry findings—two gold crimp ends with loop; one gold spring ring with jump ring; and one gold tag with jump ring (optional)
Needle-nose pliers (optional)
White (tacky) glue
Straight pins
Scissors

Finished Size: Necklace measures about 1-3/4 inches wide x 24-1/2 inches long.

Directions:
Trace patterns at right onto tracing paper with pencil.

Cut two bulb shapes from turquoise, green, purple, orange, yellow and red felt. From gold felt, cut 12 base pieces.

Referring to pattern for position, glue a base piece with right side up to the right side of each bulb piece. Let dry.

With wrong sides together and edges matching, pin matching color bulbs together.

Separate black six-strand floss and thread embroidery needle with three strands of floss. Blanket-stitch around the entire outside of a lightbulb, stuffing the bulb portion only as you stitch around.

Then add a long straight stitch across the bottom of the base of the lightbulb. See Fig. 1 below for stitch illustrations. Repeat with remaining bulbs.

Thread a pony bead onto center of black cording. Referring to photo above left for placement and making sure gold bead is centered, glue the back of the base of the orange and purple bulbs to the cording. Add a gold pony bead to each end of the cording.

Glue the remaining bulbs to the cording, separating them by gold pony beads. Let dry.

Add three gold pony beads to each end of the cording. Then tie a knot close to last bead on each end of the cording.

Tie ends of cording in an overhand knot. Or use needle-nose pliers to attach a crimp end to each end of the cording. Then add the spring ring to the loop on one end, and add the jump ring and tag to the loop on the other end.

Don this gala accent for any happy holiday gathering! ☆

FELT TREE BULB NECKLACE
Trace 1—each piece
Cut 12—gold felt
Cut 2—turquoise, green, purple, orange, yellow and red felt

Fig. 1

Blanket stitch

Long straight stitch

APPLIQUE KEY
- - - Outline/Cutting line
—— Overlapped portion of pattern

Cozy Up to Christmas with Quick-to-Crochet Afghan

NO ONE will mind if the weather outside is frightful…as long as this cuddly Christmas-colored afghan is close at hand.

Crochet designer Sharon Zimmerman of Bogota, New Jersey says, "This cheery throw makes a great project for beginners and a quick last-minute gift idea." So put on some carols, grab a cup of hot cocoa…and get busy!

Materials Needed:
4-ply worsted-weight yarn—three 8-ounce skeins of red and one 8-ounce skein each of green and white (Sharon used Red Heart Super Saver yarn in Cherry Red, Paddy Green and White)
Size J/10 (6mm) crochet hook
Scissors

Special Stitches:
V-STITCH (V-st): Dc, ch 1, dc in same st or sp indicated.

SHELL (SH): Dc, sc, dc in same st or sp indicated.

Finished Size: Afghan is 60 inches wide x 54 inches long.

Directions:
With White, ch 152.

Row 1: Dc in fourth ch from hk and in each remaining ch across, turn: 150 dcs.

Row 2: Ch 3 (counts as first dc here and throughout), dc in each remaining dc across, dc in top of turning ch, turn: 150 dcs.

Row 3: Ch 3, dc in each remaining dc across, dc in top of turning ch. Fasten off White and change to Paddy Green, turn: 150 dcs.

Row 4: With Paddy Green, ch 3, dc in next dc, * sk 2 dcs, V-st in next dc; repeat from * across to last 4 sts, sk next 2 dcs, dc in next dc, dc in top of turning ch, turn: 48 V-sts and 4 dcs.

Row 5: Ch 3, dc in next dc, * V-st in next ch-1 sp; repeat from * across to last

dc, dc in last dc, dc in top of turning ch. Fasten off Paddy Green and change to White, turn: 48 V-sts and 4 dcs.

Row 6: With White, ch 3, work 2 dcs in next dc, dc in each dc and ch-1 sp across to last 2 dcs, work 2 dcs in next dc, dc in top of turning ch, turn: 150 dcs.

Rows 7-8: Ch 3, dc in next dc and each remaining dc across, dc in top of turning ch. Fasten off White and change to Paddy Green, turn: 150 dcs.

Rows 9-10: Repeat Rows 4-5.

Rows 11-13: Repeat Rows 6-8. Fasten off White and change to Cherry Red at end of Row 13.

Row 14: With Cherry Red, ch 3, dc in next dc, sk next 2 dcs, SH in next dc, * sk next 2 dcs, SH in next dc; repeat from * across to last 4 sts, sk 2 dcs, dc in last dc, dc in top of turning ch, turn: 48 SH and 4 dcs.

Row 15: Ch 3, work 2 dcs in next dc, * SH in sc of next SH; repeat from * across, work 2 dcs in last dc, dc in top of turning ch: 48 SH and 6 dcs.

Row 16: Ch 3, dc in next dc, sk 1 dc, * SH in sc of next SH; repeat from * across to last 3 sts, sk 1 dc, dc in next dc, dc in top of turning ch: 48 SH and 4 dcs.

Rows 17-71: Repeat Rows 15 and 16, ending with a Row 15. Fasten off Cherry Red at end of Row 71 and change to White: 48 SH and 6 dcs.

Row 72: With White, ch 3, dc in each remaining st across, dc in top of turning ch, turn: 150 dcs.

Rows 73-74: Ch 3, dc in each dc across, dc in top of turning ch. Fasten off White at end of Row 74 and change to Paddy Green: 150 dcs.

Rows 75-76: Repeat Rows 4-5. Fasten off Paddy Green at end of Row 76 and change to White.

Rows 77-79: Repeat Rows 6-8. Fasten off White at end of Row 79 and change to Paddy Green.

Rows 80-81: Repeat Rows 4-5. Fasten off Paddy Green at end of Row 81 and change to White.

Rows 82-84: Repeat Rows 6-8. Fasten off White at end of Row 84.

Weave in all loose ends.

Toss over the sofa or on a bed in the guest room for a warm Christmas touch!

ABBREVIATIONS

ch(s)	chain(s)
dc(s)	double crochet(s)
hk	hook
sc(s)	single crochet(s)
sk	skip
sp(s)	space(s)
*	Instructions following asterisk are repeated as directed.

Santa Bag Puts a Fun Face on Gift-Giving

YOUNGSTERS will love making this adorable gift sack for a teacher's gift or special holiday present. Bertha Taylor of Schulter, Oklahoma designed it using easily available supplies like paper bags and paper plates, so it's ideal for group crafting as well.

"You can't help feeling like one of Santa's elves filling this bag with Christmas goodies, homemade cookies or presents from your pantry," Bertha adds.

Materials Needed:
Patterns below right
Tracing paper and pencil
Compass
8-inch x 10-inch brown paper gift bag
Two 8-inch white paper plates
10-inch square of red felt for hat and mouth
Scrap of black felt for eyes
1/2-inch red pom-pom for nose
Straight pins
Ruler
White (tacky) glue
Scissors

Finished Size: Paper bag Santa is about 8 inches wide x 10-3/4 inches high without handles.

Directions:
Trace mustache pattern at right onto folded tracing paper. Cut out shape on traced lines. Unfold for complete pattern.

Use compass to draw two 1/2-in. circles for eye patterns and one 1-in. semicircle for mouth pattern. Also draw a 1-1/2-in. circle for hat pom-pom pattern.

Referring to Fig. 1, draw hat pattern onto tracing paper with pencil.

Pin hat and mouth patterns to red felt and eye patterns to black felt. Cut out each.

Use pencil and ruler to draw a line across the center of the back of each paper plate.

Cut a 1-in.-wide piece from center of one paper plate for hat trim piece. Save remaining pieces for bottom and middle layers of beard.

Referring to Fig. 2, cut upper beard from remaining paper plate. Then cut a wide "V" shape from the straight edge of the beard piece. Discard shaded area.

Trace around mustache and pom-pom patterns onto remaining piece of paper plate with pencil. Cut out each shape on drawn lines.

Make 1-1/2-in.-long cuts 1/4 in. apart along curved edge of each beard piece.

Make 1/2-in.-long cuts 1/4 in. apart around outside edges of hat trim and pom-pom pieces.

ASSEMBLY: Place folded gift bag right side up on a flat surface. Refer to photo as a guide while assembling the Santa face as directed in the instructions that follow.

Starting about 1/2 in. from bottom edge of bag, glue bottom, middle and upper beard pieces right side up to the front of gift bag, overlapping them as shown. Let dry.

Glue red felt mouth centered above top edge of top beard piece. Let dry.

Glue mustache centered above top edge of mouth. Let dry.

Glue red pom-pom nose centered above mustache and black felt eyes above nose. Let dry.

Glue 7-in.-long edge of felt hat centered across the top edge of the upper beard piece. Let dry.

Fold tip of hat to right-hand edge of hat trim and glue to hold. Glue white pom-pom trim to tip of hat. Let dry.

Being careful not to cut the gift bag, trim side edges of beard even with side edges of the gift bag.

Stuff your Santa sack with a holiday surprise for someone special! ☆

PAPER BAG SANTA PATTERN

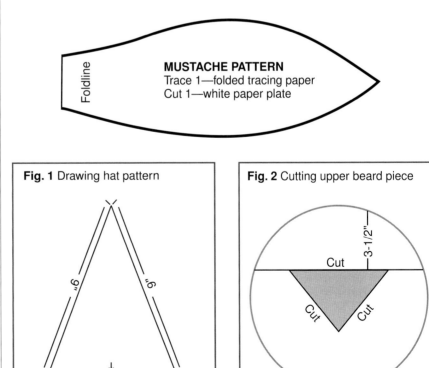

MUSTACHE PATTERN
Trace 1—folded tracing paper
Cut 1—white paper plate

Foldline

Fig. 1 Drawing hat pattern

9" 9"

7"

Fig. 2 Cutting upper beard piece

3-1/2"

Cut

Cut Cut

Cute Country Angel Spreads Holiday Spirit

HARK! This adorable herald angel has wings spread wide with her tidings of great joy. Follow Pella, Iowa crafter Lenora Schut's easy instructions to paint the cute country cherub for yourself or a friend.

"The box makes a great holiday gift container," Lenora suggests, "or a lovely gift all by itself for teachers or babysitters—any time of year."

Materials Needed:
Pattern on next page
Tracing paper and pencil
Graphite paper
Stylus or dry ballpoint pen
7-1/2-inch-wide x 4-1/2-inch-high hexagonal papier-mache box
Foam plate or palette
Paper towels
Water container
Acrylic craft paints (Lenora used DecoArt Americana)—Dark Pine, French Mauve, Hi-Light Flesh, Lamp Black, Marigold, Raw Sienna and Warm White
Paintbrushes—1/4-inch flat and

1/2-inch flat
1-inch foam brush
Ruler
Cotton swab
Toothpick
Black fine-line permanent marker
Brown colored pencil
Matte spray finish

Finished Size: Painted angel box is 4-1/2 inches high x 7-1/2 inches wide.

Directions:
Trace pattern at right onto tracing paper with pencil.

PAINTING: Keep paper towels and a basin of water handy to clean paintbrushes. Place dabs of each paint color onto foam plate or palette as needed. Add coats of paint as needed for complete coverage. Let paint dry after each application.

Refer to photo and pattern as a guide while painting as directed in the instructions that follow.

Use 1-in. foam brush and Dark Pine to paint top and sides of box lid.

Use 1-in. foam brush and Marigold to

paint sides of box bottom.

Use 1/2-in. flat brush and Dark Pine to paint two rows of 1/2-in. squares, creating a checkerboard pattern about 3/4 in. from bottom edge of box bottom.

Place angel pattern on top of box lid. Slip graphite paper between pattern and lid. Use stylus or dry ballpoint pen to retrace lines of pattern, transferring pattern onto box lid.

Use 1/2-in. flat brush and Warm White to paint wings.

Use 1/2-in. flat brush and Hi-Light Flesh to paint face, hands and feet.

Use 1/2-in. flat brush and Marigold to paint pinafore and dress.

Use 1/4-in. flat brush and Raw Sienna to paint hair.

Use 1/4-in. flat brush and Marigold to paint bow.

Use 1/4-in. flat brush and Dark Pine to paint button and to add plaid design to sleeves and bottom of dress.

Dip cotton swab into French Mauve and dab on two dots for cheeks.

Dip end of paintbrush handle into Lamp Black and dab on two small dots for eyes.

Dip toothpick into Warm White and dab a tiny dot in each eye and three tiny dots in each cheek.

Dip toothpick into Lamp Black and add two tiny dots to button. In same way, add tiny dots in groups of three to bow.

Dip toothpick into Marigold and use to draw a thin line between the two dots on the button for thread.

FINISHING: Spray box lid and bottom with matte finish following manufacturer's instructions. Let dry.

Use black permanent marker to outline angel and to add remaining black detail lines where shown on pattern.

Use brown colored pencil to add shading to pinafore, bow, feet and under sleeves.

Use as a gift box...or as a pretty Christmas accent. ✫

Painting Tips

● Use a copy machine to reduce or enlarge the pattern for use on smaller or larger boxes.

● It is not necessary to trace over every detail on the pattern. Just transfer the main outlines of the angel for a more natural look.

● Clean foam brushes with soap and water.

● Store clean paintbrushes in a container that keeps the bristles from bending.

Paper Star

TRIMS IN A TWINKLING! These super simple paper stars are sprinkled all through our book. You'll find them in gold on the cover and in bright table trims on page 100. Make your own!

Materials Needed (for one):
8-inch x 8-inch piece of tissue paper
Ruler
Stapler
Transparent tape
Scissors

Finished Size: Paper star measures about 7-1/2 inches across.

Directions:
Place tissue paper on flat surface. Starting on one straight edge, fold tissue paper into four 1-in.-wide accordion pleats (see Fig. 1).

Fold pleated paper in half crosswise. Open and staple along crease of fold.

Referring to Fig. 2 below, cut each end of the pleated paper diagonally to form the points of the star.

Fan out the pleats so the adjoining sides meet. Tape the straight edges together to hold the star shape as shown in Fig. 3. ✫

PAINTED ANGEL BOX PATTERN
Trace 1—tracing paper
Paint as directed in instructions

Fig. 1
Pleating
tissue paper

Fig. 2
Cutting points
of star

Fig. 3
Taping straight
edges

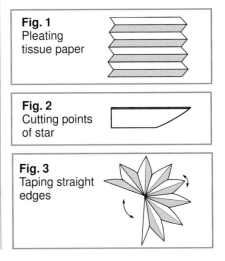

Elegant Beaded Muffler Puts The Wrap on Yuletide Chills

MAKE IT a Christmas to remember for someone special. There'll be no mistaking your warm feelings with this classy but cozy beaded muffler.

"It couldn't be quicker or easier to crochet," comments designer Tammy LeBlanc of Geismar, Louisiana. "And the few simple beads add so much...I think it's just irresistible!"

Materials Needed:
Three 6-ounce skeins with 185 yards per skein of blue bulky-weight yarn (Tammy used Lion Brand Homespun yarn in Colonial)
Size J/10 (6mm) crochet hook or size needed to obtain correct gauge
Matte finish pony beads—eight each of light blue, off-white and black
Yarn or tapestry needle
Ruler or measuring tape
Scissors

Gauge:
10 dcs and 5 rows = 4 inches. Slight variations in gauge will change the finished size a bit.

Finished Size: Scarf is about 11-1/2 inches wide x 68 inches long without fringe.

Directions:
Row 1: Ch 30, work 1 dc in fourth ch from hk and in each remaining ch across, turn: 27 dcs.

Rows 2-4: Ch 3, work 1 dc in each dc across, turn: 27 dcs.

Row 5: Ch 2, work 1 hdc in each dc across, turn: 27 hdcs.

Row 6: Ch 1, sc in first hdc, * ch 3, sk 1 hdc, insert hk into next hdc, yo and pull up a lp, carefully remove hk and thread lp through a pony bead, replace lp of yarn on crochet hk and draw lp through to complete the sc; repeat from * adding a total of 12 beads and alternating the colors of the beads across to last two hdcs, ch 3, sk next hdc, sc in last hdc, turn: 13 ch-3 sps.

Row 7: Ch 2, hdc in first sc, work 2 hdcs in each ch-3 sp across, work 1 hdc in last sc, turn: 27 hdcs.

Row 8: Ch 3, work 1 dc in each hdc across, turn: 27 dcs.

Row 9: Ch 2, work 1 hdc in each dc across, turn: 27 hdcs.

Row 10: Repeat Row 6: 13 ch-3 sps.

Row 11: Repeat Row 7: 27 hdcs.

Row 12: Repeat Row 8: 27 dcs.

Rows 13-85: Ch 3, work 1 dc in each dc across, turn: 27 dcs.

Row 86: Ch 1, sl st in each dc across. Fasten off.

Use tapestry or yarn needle to weave in loose ends.

Fringe: Cut eighty-four 12-inch-long pieces of yarn.

Working with three strands as one, fold yarn in half.

Insert crochet hk into first st of one narrow end of scarf. Draw fold of yarn through st to make a lp. Bring yarn ends through lp and pull ends to tighten lp around yarn.

In the same way, add yarn fringe to every other st at both narrow ends of the scarf.

Trim yarn ends even. ☆

ABBREVIATIONS

ch(s)	chain(s)
dc(s)	double crochet(s)
hdc(s)	half double crochet(s)
hk	hook
lp	loop
sc(s)	single crochet(s)
sl st	slip stitch
sk	skip
sp(s)	space(s)
yo	yarn over
*	Instructions following asterisk are repeated as directed.

A Lead on Beading

When adding beads, insert a small crochet hook through a pony bead, catch the loop of yarn and pull it through the bead and onto the working crochet hook. Then complete the stitch as directed.

Or, thread all the beads onto the yarn before starting to crochet, alternating the colors. Then slide a bead up to the crochet hook before working each single crochet stitch where directed.

'Paperwork' Rolls Out Pretty Accents for Christmas Boughs

DREAMING OF a white Christmas? Then you'll want to whip up a flurry of these delicate snowflakes to dangle in front of frosted windowpanes or tie on packages and the tree!

The pretty quilled ornament was designed by Cynthia Catto from Barre, Vermont.

"Once you get the hang of rolling and shaping the paper strips, you'll want to curl up and make a snowy drift of these trims," Cynthia says.

Materials Needed:
*1/8-inch-wide white quilling paper or white construction paper cut into 1/8-inch-wide strips
Corsage pin, round toothpick or quilling tool for rolling paper
Ruler
Pencil
Straight pin or toothpick
Clear-drying craft glue
5-inch square of waxed paper
8-inch length of white thread for hanging loop
Scissors*

Finished Size: Quilled snowflake ornament measures about 2-3/8 inches across without hanging loop.

Directions:
BASIC QUILLING INSTRUCTIONS:
To roll paper coils, tear off a strip of 1/8-in.-wide quilling or construction paper to the length specified in the instructions.

Moisten one end of the strip slightly and press it onto the center of the corsage pin or toothpick. If using a quilling tool, place the paper end in the crevice.

Roll the remaining length of the strip tightly between your thumb and forefinger, keeping strip's edges even. Slide pin/toothpick/tool out and glue end in place, or allow coil to open to desired size, then glue end in place. Strive for uniformity between like shapes.

When gluing quilled shapes together, use a straight pin or toothpick to place a drop of glue wherever the shapes touch.

The following shapes are used as shown in Fig. 1 at right.

Marquise: Roll a tight circle of paper around tool without gluing end. Slip paper off the tool and let it expand to 1/4 in. Glue the end. Let dry. Pinch circle on opposite sides to points.

Closed V-scroll: Crease strip at center. Glue the paper strips together 1 in. from crease. Then roll remaining ends toward crease on outside of paper.

SNOWFLAKE: Create coils as directed in instructions that follow. Lengths given represent lengths of paper strips to tear, not lengths or widths of rolled shapes.

Tear twelve 6-in. lengths of paper. Form each into a marquise shape.

Tear six 3-in. lengths of paper. Form each into a closed V-scroll.

ASSEMBLY: Place square of waxed paper on a flat surface.

Referring to Fig. 2 below, glue six marquise shapes together like spokes of a wheel. Let dry.

Referring to Fig. 3 below, glue a closed V-scroll between each marquise shape. Let dry.

Referring to Fig. 4 below, glue a marquise shape between the coils of each closed V-scroll. Let dry.

FINISHING: Carefully remove snowflake ornament from waxed paper.

Insert one end of thread through center of one outer marquise shape. Tie ends of thread together in an overhand knot for hanger. Trim ends of thread close to knot.

Hang on a tree bough or use to brighten a gift package! ✩

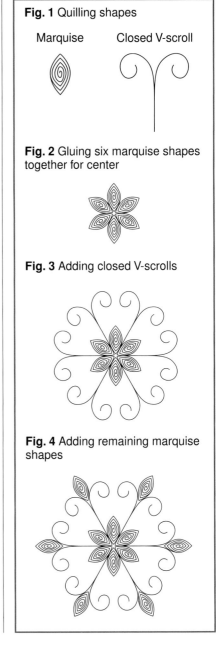

Fig. 1 Quilling shapes

Marquise   Closed V-scroll

Fig. 2 Gluing six marquise shapes together for center

Fig. 3 Adding closed V-scrolls

Fig. 4 Adding remaining marquise shapes

Vintage Mini Quilt Celebrates Christmas Past

JUST IN THE NICK of time! "Here comes a weary St. Nicholas at the end of a busy night," explains designer Marjorie Carano from West Orange, New Jersey. "He has one more stop to make, setting up this tree and placing the little sled under it."

In the spirit of the season, Marjorie added a tiny lantern to her old-time appliqued wall hanging to help light the jolly old elf's way.

Materials Needed:

Patterns on next page
Tracing paper and pencil
44-inch-wide 100% cotton or cotton-blend fabrics—1/2 yard each of beige solid for background and dark green print for backing, tree and outer border; 1/8 yard or scraps each of red print for inner border and sled; dark gold print for Santa's sack; light gold print for star; burgundy print for Santa's robe; white solid for beard, mustache and lantern; flesh solid for face; and black solid for lantern
Scrap of off-white fleece for trim on robe
Scrap of beige Ultrasuede or beige solid cotton fabric for hands
14-inch x 16-inch piece of muslin
14-inch x 16-inch piece of lightweight quilt batting
Black all-purpose thread and thread to match fabrics
Rotary cutter and mat (optional)
Quilter's marking pen or pencil
Quilter's ruler
Black six-strand embroidery floss
Embroidery needle
Yellow permanent marker
Two plastic curtain rings for hangers
Standard sewing supplies

Finished Size: Santa wall hanging is 14 inches wide x 12 inches high.

Directions:

Trace patterns on next page onto tracing paper with pencil.

With grainlines matching, pin patterns to right side of fabrics as indicated on patterns. Cut out each shape.

Use either quilter's marking pen and ruler to mark the fabrics before cutting them with a scissors, or use rotary cutting tools to cut the pieces as directed in instructions that follow. Cut the strips crosswise from selvage to selvage.

From beige solid, cut a 14-in. x 12-in. piece for appliqued background.

Place muslin piece on a flat surface. Center batting on top of muslin and beige solid background piece right side

up on top of batting. Pin corners and edges as needed to hold.

Referring to photo above as a guide, pin shapes to right side of beige background piece, overlapping the shapes as shown on patterns and leaving at least 1/2 in. around edges of background.

Use quilter's marking pen or pencil to draw runners under sled and to add inside design lines on Santa's robe freehand.

Using matching thread and narrow satin stitch, applique exposed edges of shapes to background in following order: face, robe, mustache, beard, robe trim pieces, white lantern piece, black lantern pieces, star, tree, Santa's sack and sled.

Using matching thread, satin-stitch over inside design lines of robe, catching straight edge of Santa's left mitten in the stitching.

Using black thread and a narrow satin stitch, stitch runners below sled.

With design centered, trim appliqued background to an accurate 13-in.-wide x 11-in.-high piece.

From red print, cut two 3/4-in. x 11-in. strips and two 3/4-in. x 13-1/2-in. strips for inner border.

From dark green print, cut a 15-in. x 13-in. piece for backing. Also cut two 1-in. x 11-1/2-in. strips and two 1-in. x 14-1/2-in. strips for outer border.

BORDERS: Do all stitching with right sides of fabrics together, edges even, matching thread and an accurate 1/4-in. seam allowance.

Sew an 11-in. red print border strip to opposite sides of the appliqued background. Open and press. In the same way, sew a 13-1/2-in. red print border strip to the top and bottom of appliqued background.

Sew an 11-1/2-in. dark green print border strip to opposite sides of inner border. Open and press. In the same way, sew a 14-1/2-in. green print border strip to top and bottom of inner border.

FINISHING: Thread embroidery needle with unseparated black floss. Insert needle into front of sled and then into Santa's left mitten and back again through the front of the sled to create a loop of floss. Knot floss on back.

In the same way, attach a loop of floss between the top of lantern and Santa's other hand.

Separate six-strand embroidery floss and thread needle with three strands. Attach a length of floss to each side of Santa's sack where shown in photo. Tie ends together in the center of the sack. Trim ends of floss as desired.

Use yellow marker to add a small flame to lantern.

ASSEMBLY: With right sides facing, center the green print backing piece on top of the appliqued background piece. Pin as needed to hold.

With a 1/4-in. seam, stitch around outside edges of outer border, leaving an opening for turning along one straight edge. Clip corners diagonally. Remove pins and turn right side out through opening. Turn raw edges of opening in. With matching thread, hand-sew opening closed.

Hand-sew a plastic curtain ring to the back of each upper corner of the wall hanging.

Hang up your mini quilt! ⭐

MINI QUILT PATTERNS

Trace 1 each piece—
tracing paper
Cut 1 each piece—
color of fabric indicated
on pattern

TREE

Grain

SANTA'S SACK

Grain

SLED

Grain

FACE

Grain

MUSTACHE

BEARD

Grain

ROBE

Grain

Grain

STAR

Grain

LANTERN

Grain

APPLIQUE KEY

—— Outline/cutting line
— Inside design lines
--- Overlapped portion of pattern
↔ Direction of grain

ROBE TRIM

Grain

Top Off Holidays with Warm Winter Knits

BUNDLE UP their overcoats and deck your darlings in this toasty hat and mitten set for wintry weather.

Designed by Bridgetown, Nova Scotia crafter Susan Robicheau and accented with merry red cables and bobbles, this snugly set is guaranteed to warm hearts and the snowy holiday season!

Materials Needed (for hat and mittens):

8 ounces of red worsted-weight yarn
Knitting needles—size 7 straight and set of four size 7 double-pointed needles or size needed to obtain correct gauge
Stitch marker
Cable needle
Measuring tape or ruler
Yarn or tapestry needle
Size H/8 (4.5mm) crochet hook
Scissors

Finished Size: Adult size Large mittens are about 7-1/2 inches long from end of ribbing to tip…and measure about 8 inches around fullest part of hand. Adult size hat has a 21-inch circumference.

Gauge: When working in St st, 16 sts and 24 rows = 4 inches.

Techniques/Stitches Used:
STOCKINETTE STITCH: St st: All RS rounds: Knit.

K 2, p 2 rib: Knit 2, purl 2 ribbing:
Round 1: * K 2, P 2; rep from * around.
All remaining Rounds: K the k sts and p the p sts.

Inc 1: K in front and back of next st.

T3B: Twist 3 back: Slip next st onto a cable needle and hold to back of work, k next 2 sts from left-hand needle, then p st from cable needle.

T3F: Twist 3 front: Slip next 2 sts onto a cable needle and hold to front of work, p the next st on left-hand needle, then k 2 sts from the cable needle.

T5B: Twist 5 back: Slip the next 3 sts onto a cable needle and hold to back of work, p next 2 sts from left-hand needle, then k 3 sts from cable needle.

MB: Make Bobble: Make 5 sts in one st as follows: [k the next st in the front lp and then in the back lp without removing it from the needle] twice, k in the front lp of the same st once more. Slip the st from the left needle.

Turn the work and p the five sts, turn the work and k the five sts.

With the left needle, pass the second, third and fourth sts one at a time over the first st and off the needle.

Slip, slip, knit: SSK: Sl next 2 sts one at a time onto right needle; insert the left needle into fronts of these 2 sts and k them tog.

Directions:
MITTENS: Right Mitten: Cuff: Cast on 32 sts. Divide sts over three double-pointed needles, placing 8 sts on first needle, 16 sts on second needle and 8 sts on third needle.

With fourth needle and being careful not to twist the sts, work in k 2, p 2 rib until piece measures 3 in.: 32 sts.

Next round, k 8 on first needle, [k 3, inc 1] three times, k 4 sts on second needle, k 8 on third needle: 35 sts.

Hand: H-Round 1: Place stitch marker between first two sts of Round and slip it from one needle to the next when reached to mark the beginning of each new round. K 8, p 6, T3B, p 1, T3F, p 6, inc 1, k 1, inc 1, k 5: 37 sts.

H-Round 2: K 8, p 6, k 2, p 3, k 2, p 6, k 10: 37 sts.

H-Round 3: K 8, p 5, T3B, p 3, T3F, p 5, inc 1, k 4, inc 1, k 4: 39 sts.

H-Round 4: K 8, p 5, k 2, p 5, k 2, p 5, k 12: 39 sts.

H-Round 5: K 8, p 5, k 2, p 2, MB, p 2, k 2, p 5, inc 1, k 6, inc 1, k 4: 41 sts.

H-Round 6: K 8, p 5, k 2, p 5, k 2, p 5, k 14: 41 sts.

H-Round 7: K 8, p 5, T3F, p 3, T3B, p 5, inc 1, k 8, inc 1, k 4: 43 sts.

H-Round 8: K 8, p 6, k 2, p 3, k 2, p 6, k 16: 43 sts.

H-Round 9: K 8, p 6, T3F, p 1, T3B, p 6, inc 1, k 10, inc 1, k 4: 45 sts.

H-Round 10: K 8, p 7, k 5, p 7, k 18.

H-Round 11: K 8, p 7, T5B, p 7, k 18.

H-Round 12: K 8, p 7, k 2, p 1, k 2, p 7, k 18.

H-Round 13: K 8, p 6, T3B, p 1, T3F, p 6, k 18.

H-Round 14: K 8, p 6, k 2, p 3, k 2, p 6, k 18.

H-Round 15: K 8, p 5, T3B, p 3, T3F, p 5, k 18.

H-Round 16: K 8, p 5, k 2, p 5, k 2, p 5, k 18.

H-Round 17: K 8, p 5, k 2, p 2, MB, p 2, k 2, p 5, k 18.

H-Round 18: K 8, p 5, k 2, p 5, k 2, p 5, place next 9 sts for thumb on stitch holder, cast on 2 sts, k 9: 38 sts.

H-Round 19: K 8, p 5, T3F, p 3, T3B, p 5, k 11.

H-Round 20: K 8, p 6, k 2, p 3, k 2, p 6, k 11.

H-Round 21: K 8, p 6, T3F, p 1, T3B, p 6, k 11.

H-Round 22: K 8, p 7, k 5, p 7, k 11.

H-Round 23: K 8, p 7, T5B, p 7, k 11.

H-Round 24: K 8, p 7, k 2, p 1, k 2, p 7, k 11.

H-Round 25: K 8, p 6, T3B, p 1, T3F, p 6, k 11.

H-Round 26: K 8, p 6, k 2, p 3, k 2, p 6, k 11.

H-Round 27: K 8, p 5, T3B, p 3, T3F, p 5, k 11.

H-Round 28: K 8, p 5, k 2, p 5, k 2, p 5, k 11.

H-Round 29: K 8, p 5, k 2, p 2, MB, p 2, k 2, p 5, k 11.

H-Round 30: K 8, p 5, k 2, p 5, k 2, p 5, k 11.

H-Round 31: K 8, p 5, T3F, p 3, T3B, p 5, k 11.

H-Round 32: K 8, p 6, k 2, p 3, k 2, p 6, k 11.

H-Round 33: K 8, p 6, T3F, p 1, T3B,

p 6, k 11.

H-Round 34: K 8, p 7, k 5, p 7, k 11.

H-Round 35: K 8, p 7, T5B, p 7, k 11.

H-Round 36: K 8, p 7, k 2, p 1, k 2, p 7, k 11: 38 sts.

H-Round 37: K 5, k2tog, k 1, p 1, p2tog, p 3, T3B, p 1, T3F, p 3, p2tog, p 1, k 1, SSK, k 8: 34 sts.

H-Round 38: K 7, p 5, k 2, p 3, k 2, p 5, k 10: 34 sts.

H-Round 39: K 4, k2tog, k 1, p 1, p2tog, p 1, T3B, p 3, T3F, p 1, p2tog, p 1, k 1, SSK, k 7: 30 sts.

H-Round 40: K 6, p 3, k 2, p 5, k 2, p 3, k 9: 30 sts.

H-Round 41: K 3, k2tog, k 1, p 1, p2tog, k 2, p 2, MB, p 2, k 2, p2tog, p 1, k 1, SSK, k 6: 26 sts.

H-Round 42: K 5, p 2, k 2, p 5, k 2, p 2, k 8: 26 sts.

H-Round 43: K 2, k2tog, k 1, p2tog, T3F, p 3, T3B, p2tog, k 1, SSK, k 5: 22 sts.

H-Round 44: K 4, p 2, k 2, p 3, k 2, p 2, k 7: 22 sts.

H-Round 45: K 1, k2tog, k 1, p2tog, T3F, p 1, T3B, p2tog, k 1, SSK, k 4: 18 sts.

K 3 sts from next needle: place 9 sts on each of two needles. Cut yarn and use tapestry or yarn needle to graft the stitches together. Fasten off.

Thumb: Pick up and k 4 sts along bottom edge of mitten at thumb opening. Place 9 sts from holder on two needles.

K around until thumb measures 2-1/4 in. or desired length: 13 sts.

K2tog around until 4 sts remain. Cut yarn. Thread yarn through remaining sts and fasten off.

Left Mitten: Cuff: Work the same as for right mitten cuff.

Hand: H-Round 1: Place stitch marker between first two sts of Round and slip it from one needle to the next when reached to mark the beginning of each new round. K 5, inc 1, k 1, inc 1, p 6, T3B, p 1, T3F, p 6, k 8: 37 sts.

H-Round 2: K 10, p 6, k 2, p 3, k 2, p 6, k 8: 37 sts.

H-Round 3: K 4, inc 1, k 4, inc 1, p 5, T3B, p 3, T3F, p 5, k 8: 39 sts.

H-Round 4: K 12, p 5, k 2, p 5, k 2, p 5, k 8: 39 sts.

H-Round 5: K 4, inc 1, k 6, inc 1, p 5, k 2, p 2, MB, p 2, k 2, p 5, k 8: 41 sts.

H-Round 6: K 14, p 5, k 2, p 5, k 2, p 5, k 8: 41 sts.

H-Round 7: K 4, inc 1, k 8, inc 1, p 5, T3F, p 3, T3B, p 5, k 8: 43 sts.

H-Round 8: K 16, p 6, k 2, p 3, k 2, p 6, k 8: 43 sts.

H-Round 9: K 4, inc 1, k 10, inc 1, p 6, T3F, p 1, T3B, p 6, k 8: 45 sts.

H-Round 10: K 18, p 7, k 5, p 7, k 8: 45 sts.

H-Round 11: K 18, p 7, T5B, p 7, k 8.

H-Round 12: K 18, p 7, k 2, p 1, k 2, p 7, k 8.

H-Round 13: K 18, p 6, T3B, p 1, T3F, p 6, k 8.

H-Round 14: K 18, p 6, k 2, p 3, k 2, p 6, k 8.

H-Round 15: K 18, p 5, T3B, p 3, T3F, p 5, k 8.

H-Round 16: K 18, p 5, k 2, p 5, k 2, p 5, k 8.

H-Round 17: K 18, p 5, k 2, p 2, MB, p 2, k 2, p 5, k 8.

H-Round 18: K 9, place 9 sts for thumb on stitch holder, cast on 2 sts, p 5, k 2, p 5, k 2, p 5, k 8: 38 sts.

H-Round 19: K 11, p 5, T3F, p 3, T3B, p 5, k 8.

H-Round 20: K 11, p 6, k 2, p 3, k 2, p 6, k 8.

H-Round 21: K 11, p 6, T3F, p 1, T3B, p 6, k 8.

H-Round 22: K 11, p 7, k 5, p 7, k 8.

H-Round 23: K 11, p 7, T5B, p 7, k 8.

H-Round 24: K 11, p 7, k 2, p 1, k 2, p 7, k 8.

H-Round 25: K 11, p 6, T3B, p 1, T3F, p 6, k 8.

H-Round 26: K 11, p 6, k 2, p 3, k 2, p 6, k 8.

H-Round 27: K 11, p 5, T3B, p 3, T3F, p 5, k 8.

H-Round 28: K 11, p 5, k 2, p 5, k 2, p 5, k 8.

H-Round 29: K 11, p 5, k 2, p 2, MB, p 2, k 2, p 5, k 8.

H-Round 30: K 11, p 5, k 2, p 5, k 2, p 5, k 8.

H-Round 31: K 11, p 5, T3F, p 3, T3B, p 5, k 8.

H-Round 32: K 11, p 6, k 2, p 3, k 2, p 6, k 8.

H-Round 33: K 11, p 6, T3F, p 1, T3B, p 6, k 8.

H-Round 34: K 11, p 7, k 5, p 7, k 8.

H-Round 35: K 11, p 7, T5B, p 7, k 8.

H-Round 36: K 11, p 7, k 2, p 1, k 2, p 7, k 8: 38 sts.

H-Round 37: K 8, SSK, k 1, p 1, p2tog, p 3, T3B, p 1, T3F, p 3, p2tog, p 1, k 5, k2tog, k 1: 34 sts.

H-Round 38: K 10, p 5, k 2, p 3, k 2, p 5, k 7: 34 sts.

H-Round 39: K 7, SSK, k 1, p 1, p2tog, p 1, T3B, p 3, T3F, p 1, p2tog, p 1, k 1, k 4, k2tog, k 1: 30 sts.

H-Round 40: K 9, p 3, k 2, p 5, k 2, p 3, k 6: 30 sts.

H-Round 41: K 6, SSK, k 1, p 1, p2tog, k 2, p 2, MB, p 2, k 2, p2tog, p 1, k 3, k2tog, k 1: 26 sts.

H-Round 42: K 8, p 2, k 2, p 5, k 2, p 2, k 5: 26 sts.

H-Round 43: K 5, SSK, k 1, p2tog, T3F, p 3, T3B, p2tog, k 2, k2tog, k 1: 22 sts.

H-Round 44: K 7, p 2, k 2, p 3, k 2, p 2, k 4: 22 sts.

H-Round 45: K 4, SSK, k 1, p2tog, T3F, p 1, T3B, p2tog, k 1, k2tog, k 1: 18 sts.

K 6 sts from next needle; place 9 sts on each of two needles. Cut yarn and use tapestry or yarn needle to graft the stitches together. Fasten off.

Thumb: Work as for right mitten.

Finishing: Weave in all loose ends.

HAT: Cast 83 sts onto straight needle.

Row 1 (WS): K 1, p across to last st, k 1: 83 sts.

Row 2: Repeat Row 1.

Row 3: Repeat Row 1.

Row 4: K across row.

Row 5: Repeat Row 1.

Row 6: K 1, * k 4, MB, k 4; repeat from * across to last st, k 1: 83 sts.

Row 7: Repeat Row 1.

Row 8: K 1, * k 2, MB, k 3, MB, k 2; repeat from * across to last st, k 1: 83 sts.

Row 9: Repeat Row 1.

Row 10: Repeat Row 6.

Row 11: Repeat Row 1.

Rows 12-14: K across row: 83 sts.

Row 15: K 1, p across to last st, k 1. Repeat Rows 14 and 15 until work measures 5 in. from beginning: 83 sts.

Crown: C-Row 1: K 1, * k 7, k2tog; repeat from * across to last st, k 1: 74 sts.

C-Row 2: K 1, p across to last st, k 1.

C-Row 3: K 1, * k 6, k2tog; repeat from * across to last st, k 1: 65 sts.

C-Row 4: Repeat C-Row 2.

C-Row 5: K 1, * k 5, k2tog; repeat from * across to last st, k 1: 56 sts.

C-Row 6: Repeat C-Row 2.

C-Row 7: K 1, * k 4, k2tog; repeat from * across to last st, k 1: 47 sts.

C-Row 8: Repeat C-Row 2.

C-Row 9: K 1, * k 3, k2tog; repeat from * across to last st, k 1: 38 sts.

C-Row 10: Repeat C-Row 2.

C-Row 11: K 1, * k 2, k2tog; repeat from * across to last st, k 1: 29 sts.

C-Row 12: Repeat C-Row 2.

C-Row 13: K 1, * k 1, k2tog; repeat from * across to last st, k 1: 20 sts.

C-Row 14: Repeat C-Row 2.

C-Row 15: K 1, * k2tog; repeat from * across to last st, k 1: 11 sts.

Cut yarn, leaving an 18-in. tail of yarn. Thread yarn onto yarn or tapestry needle and insert needle through remaining sts. Draw yarn up and fasten off.

With right sides facing, sew back seam of hat using yarn or tapestry needle and matching yarn. Fasten off.

Using crochet hook, sc around the bottom edge of hat. Fasten off.

Weave in all loose ends. ★

ABBREVIATIONS

k	knit
lp	loop
p	purl
RS	right side
sc	single crochet
sl	slip
st(s)	stitch(es)
tog	together
WS	Wrong side
* [ ]	Instructions following asterisk are repeated as directed.

Cross-Stitched Card Will Send a Noteworthy Noel

HANDMADE from the heart, here's a keepsake card that will post a memorable Christmas message for all the special friends on your list.

Cross-stitched by Rosella Kreuzer of Mankato, Minnesota, the simple sentiment, baby and star spell out the true meaning of the season.

"These cards work up so quickly," Rosella confirms. "You might also frame the finished design for a small gift or ornament."

Materials Needed:
Chart below
5-inch square of off-white 18-count Aida cloth
Purchased 4-1/4-inch x 5-1/2-inch blank red card with 3-inch circle window opening and matching envelope
4-inch x 5-1/4-inch piece of white paper
DMC six-strand embroidery floss in colors listed on color key
Size 14 tapestry needle
White (tacky) glue
Scissors

Finished Size: Card measures 5-1/2 inches high x 4-1/4 inches wide. The design area is 48 stitches high x 27 stitches wide and measures about 1-1/2 inches wide x 2-5/8 inches high.

Directions:
Zigzag or overcast edges of Aida cloth to prevent fraying. Fold Aida cloth in half lengthwise and then in half crosswise to determine center and mark this point.

To find center of chart, draw line across chart connecting opposite arrows. Begin stitching at this point so design will be centered.

Working with 18-in. lengths of six-strand floss, separate strands and use two strands for full and partial cross-stitching. Use one strand of red floss for backstitching lettering and one strand of gold metallic for backstitching halo and for star (eyelet stitch). See Fig. 1 for stitch illustrations.

Each square on chart equals one stitch worked over a set of fabric threads. Use colors indicated on color key to complete cross-stitching, then backstitching.

Do not knot floss on back of work.

Instead, leave a short tail of floss on back of work and hold in place while working the first few stitches over it. To end a strand, run needle under a few neighboring stitches in back before cutting floss close to work.

ASSEMBLY: With design centered, trim Aida cloth to a 4-in. x 5-in. piece.

Center cross-stitched design on inside of card behind window opening. Apply a thin bead of glue to Aida cloth near edges of window opening to attach design to card.

Glue white paper centered behind design area on inside of card. Let dry.

CROSS-STITCH NATIVITY CARD CHART

COLOR KEY	DMC
■ Red	321
▨ Very Light Brown	435
▩ Holiday Green	699
□ Topaz	725
▧ Very Light Peach Flesh	948
BACKSTITCH	
▬ Red (1 strand)	321
▬ Gold Metallic (1 strand)	5282
EYELET STITCH	
▬ Gold Metallic (1 strand)	5282

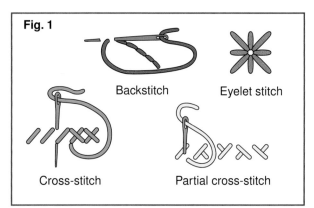

Fig. 1

Backstitch Eyelet stitch

Cross-stitch Partial cross-stitch

Birds of a Feather Flock to Merry Mitts

LOOKING FOR a creative way to use up all those scraps of fleece and bits of ribbon on hand from Christmas gifts past?

Let your imagination take wing with these pretty bird-and-mitten ornaments from Bette Veinot of Bridgewater, Nova Scotia. "They're so quick and fun to make. Just add whatever you have on hand for special sparkle," she suggests.

Materials Needed (for one ornament):

Pattern below right
Tracing paper and pencil
7-inch x 4-1/2-inch piece of solid or print Polarfleece in color of choice for mitten
2-inch x 5-inch piece of matching ribbed or print Polarfleece for cuff
Thread to match fabrics
Polyester stuffing
2-inch artificial bird in color of choice
6-inch length of gold metallic cord for hanging loop
1/2-inch-high coordinating star, sequin or heart for trim on cuff
Coordinating small artificial berries and leaves for top of mitten
8-inch length of 1/8-inch-wide coordinating ribbon for bow
Glue gun and glue sticks
Standard sewing supplies

Finished Size: Each mitten ornament measures about 3-1/2 inches across by 5 inches high without hanging loop.

Directions: Trace mitten pattern at right onto tracing paper with pencil.

Cut out two mitten pieces from 7-in. x 4-1/2-in. piece of Polarfleece, reversing one.

With right sides facing and edges matching, sew around mitten with a 1/4-in. seam, leaving straight edge open where shown on pattern. Clip curves.

Turn mitten right side out and stuff firmly with stuffing.

For hanging loop, fold gold cord in half and knot close to ends. Glue knot centered on inside top edge of one side (back) of mitten.

For cuff, fold long edges of 2-in. x 5-in. piece of ribbed or print Polarfleece to wrong side with edges meeting in the center to make a 1-in. x 5-in. piece. Glue as needed to hold.

Fold cuff piece in half crosswise and mark fold. Pin cuff right side out to top of mitten with fold mark centered on front of mitten and short ends meeting at the back. Glue cuff around top of mitten, overlapping the top edge of the mitten

about 1/2 in. Let dry.

Referring to photo for position, glue bird, berries and leaves to top of mitten. Glue star, sequin or heart trim to front of cuff. Let dry.

Tie 8-in. length of ribbon into a small bow. Referring to photo for position, glue bow to front of mitten. Let dry.

Perch on your Christmas pine or tie on gift packages! ✬

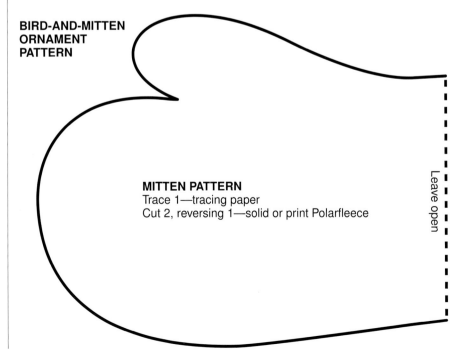

BIRD-AND-MITTEN ORNAMENT PATTERN

MITTEN PATTERN
Trace 1—tracing paper
Cut 2, reversing 1—solid or print Polarfleece

Leave open

Feliz Navidad Party!

Set the scene for a festive south-of-the-border caroling party with a table as warm and colorful as Latino Christmas traditions.

LOOKING FOR a colorful new decorating idea for this year's caroling party? Why not head south of the border for some Feliz Navidad flair?

We traded in our traditional trims of red and green for bouquets of tissue-paper flowers in warm sun-kissed orange, yellow and red (easy directions on page 91). A serape or Mexican print fabric made a festive tablecloth, with terra-cotta tiles for trivets and bright peppers (see photo at right) for candle holders.

(We even glued invitations to packs of taco seasoning mix!)

Carolers can warm up their voices with a chorus of Feliz Navidad (below right) while you warm up a hearty "Santa" Fe Chili and mugs of steaming Mexican Hot Cocoa. The cinnamon aroma of this whipped cream-topped beverage will fill your whole hacienda with a wonderful holiday scent and spirit!

Finally, for a "smashing" finale to the festivities, let blindfolded guests take a whack at a cute candy-filled snowman pinata (see page 103 for directions).

MEXICAN HOT COCOA
Stella Gilbertson, Northfield, Minnesota

12 cups water
3 to 4 cinnamon sticks (3 inches)
2 cans (16 ounces *each*) chocolate syrup
3 cans (12 ounces *each*) evaporated milk
1 can (14 ounces) sweetened condensed milk
1-1/2 teaspoons vanilla extract
Whipped cream, ground cinnamon and cinnamon sticks, optional

In a large kettle, bring the water and cinnamon sticks to a boil. Reduce heat; cover and simmer for 10-15 minutes or until liquid turns light brown. Remove cinnamon sticks.

In a large bowl, combine the chocolate syrup, evaporated milk, condensed milk and vanilla; slowly stir into cinnamon water. Simmer just until heated through. Ladle into mugs. Garnish with whipped cream, cinnamon and cinnamon sticks if desired. **Yield:** about 5 quarts.

SANTA FE CHILI
Laura Manning, Lilburn, Georgia

2 pounds ground beef
1 medium onion, chopped
2 cans (16 ounces *each*) kidney beans, rinsed and drained
2 cans (15 ounces *each*) black beans, rinsed and drained
2 cans (15 ounces *each*) pinto beans, rinsed and drained
2 cans (11 ounces *each*) shoepeg corn, drained
1 can (14-1/2 ounces) diced tomatoes, undrained
1 can (10 ounces) diced tomatoes with mild green chilies, undrained
1 can (11-1/2 ounces) V8 juice
2 envelopes ranch salad dressing mix
2 envelopes taco seasoning
Sour cream, shredded cheddar cheese and tortilla chips, optional

In a large skillet, cook beef and onion over medium heat until meat is no longer pink; drain. Transfer to a 5-qt. slow cooker. Stir in the beans, corn, tomatoes, V8 juice, salad dressing mix and taco seasoning. Cover and cook on high for 4 hours or until heated through. Serve with sour cream, cheese and tortilla chips if desired. **Yield:** 4 quarts (16 servings).

BELL PEPPERS come in a festive range of red, orange, yellow and green. Choose the color that looks best with your table. Cut stem and 1/2 inch off top of pepper. Remove membrane and seeds inside. Cut top edge in zigzag pattern. If necessary, cut a thin slice off the bottom so the pepper sits flat. Place a tealight candle in each of the pepper centers.

Feliz Navidad

Feliz Navidad

Feliz Navidad

Feliz Navidad

Prospero Año y Felicidad

REPEAT

I wanna wish you a Merry Christmas

I wanna wish you a Merry Christmas

I wanna wish you a Merry Christmas

From the bottom of my heart

REPEAT

Pinatas Pack Presents and Tradition into Holiday Times

By Stacy Johnson of Missouri City, Texas

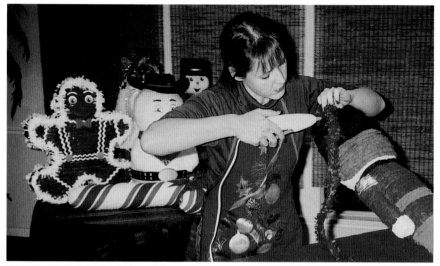

"I MAKE PINATAS all year-round, but spring and summer are my busiest seasons," Stacy says.

FAMILY TRADITIONS ARE a treasured part of Christmas celebrations in homes across the country, and though we may not realize it at the time, they're a precious gift in themselves.

At least they proved to be that for me—and for my family.

Years ago, when I was 8, my older sister asked me to help her make a papier-mache snowman pinata for a holiday art class project. She showed me how to mix and apply the newspaper, water and flour over balloons, then decorate it with crepe paper and fill it with small gifts. Our pinata was a "smashing" success—and so much fun that

we began making one for our family every year after that!

Even after I married my husband, Jerry, and was living in Missouri City, Texas with a daughter, Jaree, of my own, I continued to make that Yuletide snowman pinata.

But as much fun as the tradition was, snowmen began to get a bit boring after so many years. So I started experimenting with other holiday icons—Santa, nutcrackers, an elf, a star, a drummer boy, the Grinch. I used everything from coffee cans and shoe boxes to wastebaskets and lamp shades for molds!

Coming up with a different figure each year became a new hobby and a fun diversion from my regular job as a piping designer for the chemical industry. And I found that my drafting/design background helped me make the dimensioned drawings and precisely proportioned molds needed for many of my unique pinata figures.

Then, during a long layoff at work several years ago, my husband suggested I put up some of my Christmas pinatas on a Web site he had recently created. The response really was amazing!

Business Boom

I soon received so many requests for pinatas that I decided to quit my longtime job just to keep up with the demand. During my first year in business,

I shipped pinatas to China, Japan, Italy, Germany, Saudi Arabia and Canada …and orders have been growing ever since.

In fact, my whole family has been involved in the business at different times. Jerry runs the Web site, and my mother, sister, daughter and nieces have all helped out during hectic periods.

I remember one time my mother and Jaree offered to pull an all-nighter with me to meet a special deadline. We were diligently working when the power went out around midnight. Determined to make that deadline, we rounded up every candle we could find and kept on until morning. We still have photos and precious memories of working in the dark all that night!

Ours is a close-knit family and we know we can always depend on each other. I guess that's why our holiday traditions are so invaluable to me—because they established a bond among us and still create memories that will last a lifetime.

While some people may see a pinata as simply newspaper and glue, I see a cherished family tradition that will live in my heart forever…and hopefully in the hearts of my descendants.

Editor's Note: *For inquiries and orders, E-mail stacy@stacysstudio.com; phone 1-281/813-3122; or visit her Web site at www.stacysstudio.com.*

WHILE PINATAS USUALLY have to be smashed to release the goodies inside, Stacy makes a gentler "pull-string version" for kids or folks who want to save or reuse their pinatas.

Make Your Own Snowman Pinata

FOLLOW Stacy Johnson's easy directions to make your own holiday pinata!

Blow up a balloon to 9 in. in diameter and knot the end for head of snowman. Blow up another balloon to 11 in. in diameter and knot the end for body of snowman.

Carefully tape the 9-in. balloon to the top of the 11-in. balloon to create the snowman shape.

Mix about 3 cups water with about 2 cups flour to make a paste the consistency of heavy whipping cream. Use whisk to make a smooth paste.

Tear (do not cut) newspapers vertically into 2-in.-wide strips. Then tear each strip in half so the strips are each half the length of a page.

Dip the strips (one at a time) into the paste, removing the excess paste by sliding the strip between your index and middle fingers.

Apply strips to balloons (one at a time) horizontally, overlapping each by about 1/2 in. Continue to apply strips in this way until both balloons are covered entirely with horizontal strips.

Add a second layer of strips vertically over the entire surface as before. Then add a third horizontal layer of strips. Let dry in an even temperature area, turning as needed for even drying.

Insert two chenille stems into the top of the back of snowman's head and twist ends together to form a hanging loop. Make sure loop is secure. If needed, add more newspaper strips to the top and let dry.

Flatten bottom of the snowman so snowman stands upright.

Following paint manufacturer's instructions, spray-paint the snowman white. Add additional coats of paint as needed. Let dry.

Cut six 24-in.-long strips of white crepe paper. Stack the strips with edges matching. Working with all the strips as one, fold the strips in half lengthwise. Using scissors, cut 1/2-in.-long slits 1/2 in. apart along the folded edge of the strips for fringe. Separate strips. Fold strips in half as before.

Starting at the bottom, glue the uncut edges of a strip around the snowman so the fringed edge is outward. In the same way, add remaining fringed white strips. Cut and fringe additional white crepe paper strips as needed and glue them in a spiral around snowman until the entire snowman is covered. Let dry.

HAT: If desired, make a black construction paper hat to fit the top of snowman's head or use a purchased hat.

Glue a red construction paper hat-

band around base of hat, overlapping ends in back.

Cut three holly leaves from green construction paper. Punch three red circles from red construction paper for berries. Glue holly leaves and berries to hatband. Let dry.

Glue hat to top of snowman's head.

FACE/BUTTONS: Referring to photo above for size, cut white and black ovals from construction paper for eyes. Glue to one side of the snowman's head.

Roll a small triangle of orange construction paper into a small cone for nose. Glue straight edge to hold cone shape. Glue nose to front of snowman below eyes. Let dry.

From black construction paper, cut five irregular circles for mouth and glue the pieces to snowman below nose.

Glue three red construction paper buttons down center front of snowman.

FINISHING: Tie a green scarf around snowman's neck. Use craft knife to cut a small three-sided flap in top back of snowman's body. Fill pinata with candy. Use paper punch to make a hole in the flap and a corresponding hole in the snowman's body. Thread curling ribbon through holes and tie ends in a bow.

Spray snowman pinata with glitter spray. Let dry. ✳

SEASONAL TREASURES sport quaint trims and celebrate both holidays and historical themes.

She Brings Spindly Santas and Christmas Characters to Life

MOST OF US must wait for Santa to visit our homes every Christmas Eve, but Lisa Tibbals runs into him all year long!

Everywhere she turns—from pillar to post—this talented folk artist finds St. Nick…as well as nutcracker soldiers, angels, snowmen, carolers and other seasonal figures hiding in wood turnings of all sizes and shapes.

They may peek out from the small spindles of an old crib or from broken chairs and farm-table legs. Sometimes

they're tucked in staircase railings, plant stand legs—even the posts from her husband's boyhood bunk bed!

But with a little paint and a lot of talent, time and detail, Lisa transforms both new and old wood scraps into sprightly spindle people—each a signed and numbered limited edition with its own unique personality.

"Sometimes it takes a couple years of looking at an odd-shaped spindle before I know what to do with it," Lisa notes from the Muskego, Wisconsin home she shares with husband Steve and daughters Sarah and Shannon. "Other times a character jumps right out at me!

"But I love the idea of recycling and preserving pieces of once beautiful furniture otherwise destined for the dump." She starts by stripping, sanding, smoothing and sealing each antique spindle before literally deciding "which end is going to be up".

Then the bottom is leveled and the spindle is mounted on a base. Missing chunks may need patching with wood filler, Lisa notes, but cracks, chips and knots only add character to a

FUN FIGURES into Lisa Tibbals' crafting of snowmen (inset), Santas and angels. "I need a creative outlet in my life," she says, "and I've gotten to meet so many nice new people."

piece that can take from 2 to 20 hours to complete.

"All painting is done freehand. Nothing—not even the check patterns and stars—are stenciled," Lisa says. "I pencil in a face area, start with the nose and work out from there, layering on acrylic paint."

The possibilities are endless, she adds. "I'm constantly coming up with new ideas that different family members or the spindles themselves suggest …or that my customers request."

The 3,000 spindle folk she's turned out in the decade since starting her American Spindle Art business are now in galleries and collections across the U.S.—as well as Japan, Australia, Canada, Sweden, Scotland, Germany and France.

And although Lisa enjoys painting all her characters, her favorite subjects remain Santas and angels.

"Santas recall the magic of my own childhood," she confides. "And angels remind me of dear friends and family whose encouragement has affected my life and the path I've chosen."

Editor's Note: *For more information, E-mail Lisa at spindlelady@wi. rr.com or call 1-414/529-3651.* ❄

A Custom-Made Christmas

By Marie Savage of Youngstown, Ohio

"I CAN'T find it!" Elizabeth practically shouted at her husband. "I can't find Grandma's kolache recipe."

Tim looked up from his paper, a slight smile on his face. She always got this way around the holidays. Elizabeth wanted everything perfect at Christmas…the tree, the decorating, the baking…*especially* the baking.

"Don't worry, hon, you'll find it. Besides, you bake the same thing every year—probably don't *need* a recipe."

Elizabeth scowled at her husband. Tim didn't understand. "*Grandma* didn't need a recipe," she said. "I do."

She could picture the kolache now, golden-brown nut and poppy seed logs on platters on her grandma's kitchen table.

Grandma had come to this country from Czechoslovakia, bringing her knowledge of old-world baking with her. She never wrote anything down but could tell if things were right just by the feel of the dough.

Elizabeth didn't have that ability. She had carefully watched her grandmother make the rolls, painstakingly writing down measurements to replace the old woman's "pinches" and "handfuls" until she'd come up with a reasonable facsimile of grandma's creation.

A Legacy Lost

When her grandmother died, Elizabeth had taken over the baking duty—not so much because she enjoyed baking, but because in a household of Slovakian ancestry, Christmas just simply wouldn't be the same without kolaches.

But now the treasured recipe was nowhere to be found.

"Why not just forget about baking this year, hon? You always say it's not your favorite thing to do," Tim said.

Elizabeth couldn't believe her ears. Tim was right, of course. She wasn't a baker at heart. She had never cared for the precise measuring and careful timing baking required. One mistake and a whole batch of cookies could be ruined.

But *not* bake kolaches for the holidays? Unthinkable!

"What are you saying, Tim?" Elizabeth demanded. "You're the first one to grab it when it comes out of the oven."

Tim kept his head buried in the newspaper. "Just thought you might save yourself the aggravation this year," he offered.

The recipe still hadn't turned up when Elizabeth talked to her daughter a few days later.

"Don't worry, Mom," Lisa said. "I'll bring your grandkids over and we'll cut out cookies together. You won't even have to bake this year."

There it was again. *For some reason, no one seems to want me near an oven*, Elizabeth thought. Maybe, after all these years, she just wasn't a good baker.

In the bustle of the season, she soon found plenty of other things to occupy her time. There were gifts to shop for and wrap, decorations to put up… And, after her grandkids spent 2 days in her kitchen cutting out dozens of cookies, every available space was covered with blue and red trees, Santas with green beards, rainbow-colored stars.

This is what the holidays should be about, thought Elizabeth, surveying her kitchen. *We should have fun instead of worrying about every detail.*

Still, she felt a pang of guilt about not upholding her grandmother's tradition this year. But after she searched every nook and cranny of her house, the kolache recipe was gone.

A few days before Christmas, Elizabeth and Tim hosted their annual family dinner. Lisa and her family would be coming, along with all the aunts, uncles and cousins.

Tim piled his granddaughters' colorful cookies on a platter. "These certainly are attention grabbers," he chuckled. Elizabeth didn't notice the empty tray he set beside them.

New Tradition Found

Soon the house was filled with the noise only a joyful family can create. Elizabeth almost didn't hear the doorbell. She answered it to find Lisa and her family, the little girls struggling to hold a big box topped with a ribbon.

"You'd better take that before they drop it," Lisa advised.

They all piled into the kitchen to watch as Elizabeth opened the box to reveal several packages wrapped in aluminum foil.

"Hurry, Grammy, open them!" The little girls were beside themselves with excitement. Even Tim was grinning from ear to ear as Elizabeth peeled back the foil. Inside each package was a golden-brown kolache log!

"Three with nuts and three with poppy seed!" Lisa exclaimed. "I think they turned out really well."

Elizabeth's eyes filled with tears.

Lisa started to laugh. "Oh, Mom, I know you don't really like to bake. Since I *do*, I thought I'd surprise you. I 'stole' your recipe last month with a little help from Dad. This will be my annual Christmas gift to you…and to Great-Grandma." ❄

CAN-DO Christmastime Magic

FRONT DOOR CANDOR is all natural—and the first festive thing to greet family and friends who come to call during the holiday season.

SANTA HIMSELF might marvel at this merry medley of crafty Christmas decorating ideas. Each transforms simple cans into simply stunning holiday trims—all through the house!

Open your door to natural elegance with a festive display like the one above. To frame the doorway, fill two large coffee cans with sand and add willowy bare branches spray-painted white.

Next, wrap pine garlands and sprigs of red berries around the branches. Wire pinecones and clear plastic beads to branches and garlands. (Strings of mini lights are another option.) Top the cans with bright red Christmas bows.

Use a glitter pen to trace gala designs on a small tin (at right). Poke a hole through opposite sides near the top of the can. Attach a handle of tiny wired stars, then fill with tulle and star candy for a pretty party favor.

Glue wired holiday ribbon around small clean cans in various sizes, covering each one completely. Fill with tiny artificial trees. Glue red beads or berries at random to the branches. March across a holiday napkin on your windowsill or mantel (opposite, top).

Using crayons or stickers and a little ingenuity, your child can go to the head of the class with a can recycled into a nifty teacher's gift (opposite page, bottom left). Also, light up a tree with reflections off tiny tins (bottom middle) or create a mini craft room (bottom right)!

CANDIDLY CLASSY is this star-studded candy cup a-glitter with silver and gold.

106

CANNERY ROW-HO-HO! Make a merry mantel or window accent in minutes with scraps of ribbon and small cans.

A CAN'T-MISS TREAT for teacher that youngsters will love to make. Wrap clean can with white paper. Trim with holiday stickers. Fill with small and tasty treats.

UNCANNILY BRIGHT. Pierce holes in sides of shallow can. Glue sheer ribbon around it. Cut small hole in bottom of can and insert mini bulb to light. Attach pretty cord to use as a hanger and dangle from a tree branch.

CANNED CRAFTER gift starts with shiny new paint can. Glue buttons and bright rickrack to decorate the outside. Fill with an assortment of necessary notions for your special crafter.

Mom's Magic Cookies

By Cherie Durbin of Hickory, North Carolina

A SPICY AROMA filled the house that Christmas Eve as Mama finished up her holiday baking. My brother, Jimmy, and I worked together at the kitchen table. Jimmy poked raisin "eyes" into warm gingerbread men, while I made paper chains for the tree.

Mama kept glancing nervously at the clock. "I wonder what's keeping your father," she said.

Daddy always waited until the very last minute to get our Christmas tree. A few years of meager crops had made money tight, and he was forever looking for ways to cut corners.

"A tree to hang frills on is a luxury," he told Mama.

Mama disagreed. They'd argue for days. But when December 24 rolled around and we still had no tree, Mama would start working harder than any elf of Santa's!

She'd wake Jimmy in the wee hours of the morning and together they'd tend to most of the daily farm chores. Then Mama would whip up a special breakfast for Daddy, carrying a tray with homemade biscuits, sausage, his newspaper and a steaming mug of coffee into the bedroom where he slept.

Daddy believed in hard work and rarely took a day off, but I think he enjoyed having Mama fuss over him. There wasn't much time for that with two kids and a farm to run!

While Daddy relaxed, Mama started making her famous chocolate chip cookies—Daddy's favorite treat. Besides the many blue ribbons they'd garnered at the county fair, we knew those cookies had also won Dad's heart.

"When your mama and I were courting," he used to relate, "I came down with the flu. Your mama brought me a plate of those cookies, warm from the oven. After just one bite, I knew she must be an angel because they were divine. So I asked her to marry me.

"Never knew if it was those cookies or her saying 'yes', but the very next day my chills were gone and I was back to work. Those are 'miracle' cookies for sure," he'd proclaim.

Invariably, once Daddy had his cook-ies, we would get our tree.

Of course, the fancier trees had been picked over by then. But no matter how flawed the fir he brought home, Mama would turn any bald spots to the wall and cover any browning needles with artificial snow. Then Jimmy and I would trim the branches with fat gingerbread men and colorful paper chains.

This Christmas was different.

Mama was just taking the last batch of cookies from the oven when Dad's truck sputtered into the driveway. Jimmy ran to open the door, but Daddy stayed outside, shivering in the cold.

"What's wrong, honey?" asked Mama, coming to the door.

"I'm afraid I missed the boat this time," he whispered. "I couldn't find a tree anywhere. All the lots sold out."

"Oh, Daddy," I wailed, "if we don't get a tree, Santa won't come because he won't have any place to leave presents."

"Now we won't even *have* a Christmas," Jimmy said sadly. "He'll probably leave the bike I asked for at Willie's house. At least he has a tree."

"There, there," Mama spoke softly. "Don't worry. Tonight we'll leave Santa some of Daddy's miracle cookies and a note explaining our situation." She flashed Daddy an angry look.

I'd been especially good that year, in hopes Santa would bring the pretty pink coat I'd seen in the department store window in town. I knew I'd never get it now and cried myself to sleep.

Christmas morning arrived. Outside my window, snow fell, blanketing the fields in white. I suddenly remembered the real reason for the holiday was to celebrate the birth of Jesus, the greatest of all miracle workers. I felt ashamed of the way I'd carried on last night.

Bouncing out of bed to share my cheer, I danced down the hall and gasped. There was the most splendid Christmas tree I'd ever seen! It was lush and sparkly with silver balls and hundreds of twinkling lights. Scattered beneath were gaily wrapped packages, and one gift too big to wrap had a red bow tied to its handlebars!

I glanced at the table where Mama had left out her miracle cookies. Sure enough, Santa had eaten every one.

"Always believe in miracles," Daddy said, handing me a fancy department-store box. "And in Santa," Mama said.

Sweet Christmastime

It's Christmas 'round the countryside—
There's goodwill everywhere;
Sleigh bells jingle loudly and
Sweet carols fill the air.

Gay shoppers, with their packages
Bedecked in ribbons bright,
Exchange the season's greetings.
Snow drapes the earth in white.

Smoke spirals lazily upward
From Yule logs burning low;
There's a secret special atmosphere
And hearts are all aglow.

Sweet Christmastime is here again,
The day we pause to remember
Whose birth it is we celebrate
At this lovely time in December.

—Lucille King
Mifflinburg, Pennsylvania

Do Guests a Favor!

Festive napkin rings double as keepsake party favors.

RING IN the holidays at Christmas dinner with this gala idea. Begin by rolling napkins so no hemmed edges are showing. Do this by folding two opposite edges in to meet at the center, making a rectangle.

Then, loosely roll each napkin, starting at one narrow end. Place on the table with the open edge down.

To trim with a reusable take-home trinket, add (left to right) a wreath of jingle bells strung on a wire. Or tuck a favorite holiday photo or wish inside a plastic key chain tied on with a bow.

Recycle a cardboard ring with jolly wrapping paper. Stuff a puff of beaded ribbon into a cute cookie cutter. Add a twist of gold cord to a bright Christmas tree bulb. Deck napkin with a shimmery beaded bracelet (see page 75 for directions)—or some holiday magic of your own!

Goat Milk Soaps and Bath Items Make Clean Sweep of Gift Lists

WHAT DOES SANTA put at the top of his Christmas wish list? The goat milk soaps and bath products that Maryclaire Mayes makes at Alabu Inc. might be a good guess.

Could there *be* anything nicer, after an icy all-night ride and layers of ashes and soot, than a hot soak and soothing handmade soaps in a sleighful of holiday scents?

Maryclaire and husband Dean, daughter Nell, 20, and son Hal, 17, have been making their rich, all-natural bars for 7 years—doubling their business just about every year.

"What started out as a home-school science project has grown into a real family enterprise," Maryclaire explains from their 36-acre farm in Mechanicville, New York.

"A girlfriend needed to get rid of some goat milk one day and suggested we make soap in her kitchen as a chemistry lesson for the kids."

That project brought back childhood memories of an uncle's homemade soap and her own longings for life in the slow lane, Maryclaire recalls. "I'd love the horse-and-buggy days when people's lives followed the rhythms of the earth. I always felt I was born a century too late."

After letting their soap "cure" for 4 weeks, she took it home, tried it and was amazed.

"Actually, my whole family was amazed," she says. "We'd never realized how drying commercial products are. This soap left our skin feeling silky soft, clean and moisturized.

"I was hooked on making my own soap. I even started giving it away as gifts," she recalls, adding that she'd always used crafting to cut holiday gift expenses—making baskets, jams and hand-dipped candles over the years.

"But the response to this soap was overwhelming. Everybody loved the stuff and wanted more!"

It was her husband who suggested she start selling her soaps and today handles the Web site with their son. Their daughter thought up the name Alabu and helps Maryclaire make, wrap and ship the soap. And her mother writes brochure descriptions for each bar, bath product and lip balm.

While milk has been used for centuries as a cleanser and beauty aid, Maryclaire explains, goat milk is especially rich in proteins, vitamins and minerals that nourish the skin. It also helps maintain the skin's natural pH balance and is wonderful for those with sensitive complexions or people who struggle with psoriasis, eczema and acne.

"Using a 'cold' process method to handcraft our soaps in small batches helps preserve these special qualities and also retains the glycerin to help skin hold its natural moisture," she says.

KITCHEN SCIENCE. A home-school lesson bubbled into a whole line of bath products.

Each 3-1/4-ounce bar contains 1 ounce of fresh pasteurized goat milk, plus cocoa butter and other essential oils—but no colors, preservatives, fillers or water.

The hand-cut bars come in 50 different scents, including Bayberry, Pine and Gingerbread—Santa's favorites!

Editor's Note: *Alabu soaps and gift baskets can be ordered on-line at www.alabu.com or by calling 1-888/ 509-7627.* ❄

CHRISTMAS scents, shapes and wrappings make Alabu soaps something to celebrate!

FAMILY SUPPORT is one secret to the success of Maryclaire's growing home-based business.

GLAD TIDINGS bring Kay Curtis and (left to right, below) her son Tim, husband Dan and daughter Charity together with church friends, faithful visitors and farm animals to celebrate the First Noel in true country style.

Country Nativity Brings Spirit And Story of Christmas to Life

WISE MEN (and women and children) still seek out the true reason for this season "away in a manger," says Kay Curtis of Guthrie, Oklahoma. "And if you build one, they will come."

She wasn't so certain of that when she first suggested putting on a living Nativity to the little country Potter Community Church where her husband preaches twice a month.

"The church is so small—with outhouses, no running water and less than a dozen members in regular attendance," Kay notes. "And because it's located 4 miles off the highway on a dirt road and 8 miles from the nearest town, I realized members might not think it was worth the effort since there was no guarantee of a good turnout."

But the church embraced the idea and began, that very night, to brainstorm how to build a stable, make costumes, where to get animals…

"Two of the men, including my husband, even decided to grow beards for a more Biblical look!" Kay laughs.

And on the night of the blessed event, some 60 people made their way to a humble stable, where they found the Holy Family amid tinsel-trimmed angels, shepherds and magi. Sheep and goats quietly munched hay beside a sleepy burro and some roosting chickens.

Inside the entry to the church, children could choose a shepherd or angel costume to wear while sitting on a hay bale before a cardboard replica of the humble stable to have a free photo taken. Above the one-room church and stable, stars and soft carols filled the sky and that Holy Night.

And as the crowd melted into the dark, Kay recalls, one woman rewarded all their efforts and echoed the joy they felt with simple praise: "This was wonderful…just so wonderful."

Editor's Note: *If you're in the area and interested in attending this annual event, call 1-405/969-2210 for date and directions.* ❄

A MANGER scene of cardboard (right) was set up so kids could try on a costume for a photo taken in front of the scene, then share some cookies and cocoa with their families.

May the music of Christmas sound a note of peace, tranquillity and joy in your hearts that lingers on throughout the year.

Index

Food

Appetizers & Snacks

Beverages

Candy

Condiments

Cookies & Bars

Desserts (also see Cookies & Bars)

Main Dishes

Muffins & Doughnuts

Quick Breads

Rolls & Sweet Rolls

Side Dishes

Soup & Salads

Yeast Breads

Crafts

Share Your Holiday Joy!

DO *YOU* celebrate Christmas in a special way? If so, we'd like to know! We're already gathering material for our next *Country Woman Christmas* book. And we need your help!

Do you have a nostalgic holiday-related story to share? Perhaps you have penned a Christmas poem…or a heartwarming fiction story?

Does your family carry on a favorite holiday tradition? Or do you deck your halls in some festive way? Maybe you know of a Christmas-loving country woman others might like to meet?

We're looking for *original* Christmas quilt patterns and craft projects, plus homemade Nativities, gingerbread houses, etc. Don't forget to include your best recipes for holiday-favorite main-dish meats, home-baked cookies, candies, breads, etc.!

Send your ideas and photos to "*CW* Christmas Book", 5925 Country Lane, Greendale WI 53129. (Enclose a self-addressed stamped envelope if you'd like materials returned.)